IN NORTH PEMBROKESHIRE

Hazards and Problems
Take Notice, Take Care

The author and the publishers stress that walkers should be aware of the dangers that may occur on all walks.

- check local weather forecast before walking; do not walk up into mist or low clouds
- use local OS maps side by side with walking guides
- wear walking boots and clothing
- do not take any unnecessary risks – conditions can change suddenly and can vary from season to season
- take special care when accompanied by children or dogs
- when walking on roads, ensure that you are conspicuous to traffic from either direction

Walks with History

Circular Walks
in
North Pembrokeshire

Paul Williams

First edition: 1997
Revised edition: 2009
© Text: Paul Williams

ISBN: 978-1-84524-129-2

Cover design: Sian Parri

First published in 1997 by Gwasg Carreg Gwalch

Revised edition published in 2009 by Llygad Gwalch,
Ysgubor Plas, Llwyndyrys, Pwllheli, Gwynedd LL53 6NG
☎ 01758 750432   ▤ 01758 750438
✆ books@carreg-gwalch.com
Web site: www.carreg-gwalch.com

**14 circular walks highlighting
Pembrokeshire's landscape beauty and heritage**

Easy directions for all walks and how to get there

Pubs and Cafes and Local Attractions

Information Centres and Youth Hostels

If you want to see and experience the best of Pembrokeshire then this is the book for you! 14 circular walks have been selected that highlight Pembrokeshire's outstanding landscape beauty and history.

Suitable for families and individuals all walks are easy to follow and clear directions are given, together with sketch maps to help you find the way. Simple directions on how to reach the start of each walk are listed, as are details of public transport.

Whether you choose to explore spectacular coastal scenery, hidden river valleys or magical Preseli uplands, or to follow in the footsteps of Neolithic settlers, Celtic saints and Norman adventurers, points of interest will explain what gives each area it's own brand of uniqueness. There is a quick reference guide to help you in your choice.

To further entice you there are pubs and cafés, wildlife parks, castles, churches and mills to visit. All Information Centres and Youth Hostels are listed, together with notes on camping and carvan sites. And if this is not enough then there are suggestions for further walks!

CONTENTS

The Walks
A. The North and the Preseli Hills (OS Maps 1:50 000 Cardigan 145; 1:25 000 Outdoor Leisure 35 North Pembrokeshire)

B. The North West and St Brides Bay (OS Maps 1:50 000 St David's and Haverfordwest 157; 1:25 000 Outdoor Leisure 35 North Pembrokeshire).

Features

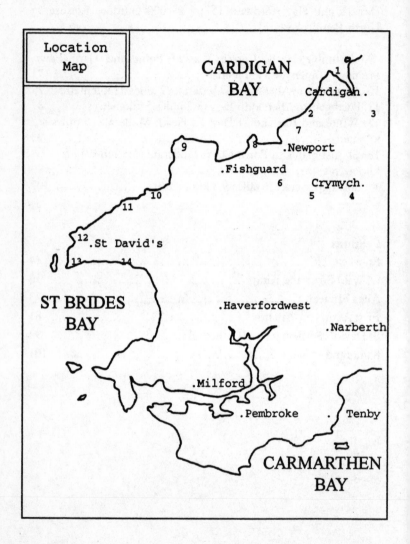

Location Map

CARDIGAN BAY

Cardigan .

1

2   3

7

9   8   .Newport

.Fishguard

10   6

11   Crymych .

5   4

12 .St David's

13   14

ST BRIDES
BAY

.Haverfordwest

.Narberth

.Milford

.Pembroke   . Tenby

CARMARTHEN
BAY

8

INTRODUCTION

Out and About

One of the aims of this guide is simplicity. Walks are easy to follow, and clear directions are given. Another aim is variety. Walks have been selected that will highlight Pembrokeshire's outstanding landscape beauty and history. The exact location for the starting point of each walk is given, and how to get there. Relevant bus routes and numbers are included — though given that Pembrokeshire is a rural area services can be infrequent; eg perhaps only on Tuesdays! Nor do all buses operate on Sundays. Train services are also noted. Check with Information Centres for full details. The National Park occasionally operate a Coast Path bus service to the more popular coastal areas. There is adequate parking space at the start of each walk — precise details are given.

Walks vary in length from 2.5 miles/4 kilometres to 11 miles/17.5 kilometres — the latter a proper hill walk to whet the appetite! The routes utilise the long distance Pembrokeshire Coast Path, public footpaths, bridleways and the occasional permissive path. They are well maintained, and clearly signposted and waymarked — a yellow arrow or waymark indicating a public footpath, a blue one a bridleway. An acorn indicates the route is a long distance path, and is often confused with the, quite separate, National Trust's logo of an oak leaf! Many people are uncertain of how long a walk of e.g. 7 miles would take. As a rough guide an average walker would expect to cover 3 miles/4 kilometres an hour over level ground, on the ascent an hour for every 2000 feet/600 metres. Sketch maps for each walk are provided — all, except Walk 5 (based on scale 1:50 000), are based on the 1:25 000 series; however they can be no substitute for the definitive OS (Ordnance Survey) maps. The 1:50 000 maroon covered Landranger series (1.25 inches = 1 mile/2 centimetres = 1 kilometre) cover the county in 3 maps: Cardigan, St David's and Haverfordwest, and Tenby. Those preferring greater detail will wish to acquire the 1:25 000 series (2.5 inches = 1 mile/4 centimetres = 1 kilometre). The yellow covered Outdoor Leisure series cover the county in 2 maps:

35 North Pemrokeshire and 36 South Pembrokeshire. The green covered Pathfinder series are more numerous, covering as they do a much smaller area per map. The relevant maps for each walk are listed.

The grading system used is largely self-explanatory. Easy walks involve short walks over easy terrain, with little variation in contour. Moderate may have 1 or 2 short steep sections, with a little more variety in landscape, whilst strenuous will involve longer distances, with, perhaps, greater sections of ascent and descent, and over different types of terrain e.g. heather, woodland paths etc. Points of interest are included which are designed to give a quick snapshot of a particular area, what gives a place in landscape and historical terms it's own brand of uniqueness. Under facilities are listed alternative parking areas — as the walks are circular they may be joined at any convenient point, and details of parking at the most accessible points are listed. Also included are the nearest BT telephones, public toilets, cafés and pubs, Post Offices and shops, youth hostels, camping and caravan sites. Most small towns and many farms will offer B & B — check with Information Centres if you are interested. A separate list of all the youth hostels in the county is given under Other Information in the Appendix. Also listed under facilities are any additional places of interest in the neighbourhood e.g. wildlife parks, castles, mills.

Finally a word of warning. Footpaths get muddy, and cliffs can be dangerous. Take care! Ensure you have adequate clothing, and the proper footwear, i.e. boots or stout shoes, for each walk. Follow the Country Code!

Landscape and Culture
Pembrokeshire — the name is an anglicisation of the Welsh *Penfro*, or Land's End — juts out into the sea at the south west corner of Wales. Surrounded on three sides by the powerhouses of the Atlantic Ocean and the Irish Sea it's spectacular cliffs are studded with glittering coves and bays. One of the essential features of this landscape is it's many isolated peninsulas; another the extraordinary flatness of the land. Only the heather clad hills of the

Preseli (home of the bluestones of Stonehenge), the great stone outcrops at Strumble Head, St David's and Treffgarne gorge, and the southern Ridgeway, rise above the uniformity. In the south, like a sword slash, the Milford Haven tears the plateau apart.

The county is renowned for it's magnificent coast and it's sandy shores, yet it has a magic and uniqueness which goes beyond these, for it is a microcosm of the major habitats to be found in Britain. The coastal waters are particularly rich in marine flora and fauna; the area around Skomer Island being designated Britain's second marine nature reserve after Lundy Island. The Dyfed coast plays host to some 5,000 grey seals; harbour porpoises and bottlenose dolphins are common sitings. The bird islands of Grassholm, Skomer and Skokholm are of international importance. Grassholm is the world's third largest gannetry, Skomer one of the world's top spots for the Manx shearwater. If razorbills and guillemots, fulmars, kittiwakes and puffins galore are main menu items then the islands are the places to visit! Fortunately the islands escaped the worst of the *Sea Empress* disaster, when in February 1996 70,000 tonnes of light crude oil were spilled into the sea from the stranded supertanker. However with oil reaching as far as Devon some thousands of oiled birds were the tragic result. Good mainland locations for birdwatchers are at Dinas Island, Strumble Head, and, in the south near Bosherston, at Stack Rocks and Stackpole Head.

Pembrokeshire's cliffs, at their highest in the north, are regal in spring and early summer. Magical yellows of gorse and bird's-foot trefoil mingle with the pinks of the thrift and the whites of sea campion. The succession of flowers continues, as if to order, from March to August. In the south are the main sand dune systems, extensive at Penally and Freshwater West, with smaller systems at Broad Haven South and Manorbier. Northern systems, some protected, are at Whitesand Bay, Newport and Poppit Sands. Sheltered behind shingle banks or sand bars are pockets of saltmarsh. Usually found at the mouths of estuaries they are hostile to all but the most salt tolerant plants. The Gann, at Pickleridge near Dale, is perhaps the most important, with others at Newport

11

and the Teifi at Cardigan. Together with intertidal mudflats, formed by the accumulation of silt where fresh and salt waters meet, they are highly important feeding grounds for thousands of overwintering waders and wildfowl. The mudflats of Angle Bay, and the western and eastern arms of the Cleddau river, are particularly popular.

Freshwater habitats include the marshes found at the flood plains of rivers and streams. Good examples are at Penally, and at Pentood Marsh in Cilgerran Wildlife Centre. The largest area of open water in the National Park are the delightful lily ponds at Bosherston, a highly popular summer venue. Llysyfran Reservoir and Country Park, opened in the 1970s, attracts a number of winter waterfowl, as well as offering water sports and fishing. Remnants of the oak forest which once covered Pembrokeshire remain. Clinging to the sides of isolated valleys and hills, and along the steeper sections of river banks, they have unique beauty and atmosphere. The Gwaun valley in it's summer yellows and greens, or with the early morning mist rising from the water, is rightly famous, whilst hidden amongst the steep oak woods of the Cleddau are Norman river castles; whitewashed Benton opposite Lawrenny, or Carew, glimpsed through the trees bordering the Carew river. Less dramatic are the uniform stands of coniferous plantations which dot the uplands.

In the north of the county are the Preseli hills, extensive areas of lowland heath, acid grassland and moorland. They are predominantly heath, dominated by heather, with gorse in western areas giving way to bilberry in the east. Patches of wet heath or bogland, with sphagnum and cotton grass, break up the landscape. Smaller areas of low lying heath are at Strumble Head and St David's Head. Roadside verges, and traditional hedgebanks, whether of stone and/or turf, are ablaze with the colours of wild flowers in spring and early summer. The semi-natural specialised grassland of farms have less to offer in terms of wildlife, though many have areas of waste ground or a pond. In the south the limestone cliffs, and the plateau, with it's short springy turf and superb maritime flora, is one of the most impressive limestone areas in Britain.

Geologically Pembrokeshire is of spectacular interest. Not only does it offer magnificently exposed rock formations around it's coast, but the series of rocks on display range in an unbroken series from the very oldest Pre-Cambrian, from 3,000 million years ago, to the Carboniferous coal measures of 300 million years ago. The Pre-Cambrian rocks, formed before the appearance of any obvious fossilized life, occur in a small area extending from Whitesand Bay to Porth Llysgi. Later Lower Palaeozoic rocks, the Cambrian, Ordovician and Silurian systems which begin 570 million years ago, occur, like the Pre-Cambrian, in the north of the county. These igneous and sedimentary rocks were faulted and folded at the end of the Silurian period, some 400 million years ago, during the great Caledonian earth movements. As a result a WSW-ENE grain was imposed across the north of the county; one further result being the formation of St David's peninsula.

By contrast the rocks in southern Pembrokeshire are mainly Upper Palaeozoic. Devonian Old Red Sandstone covers most of the north side of Milford Haven, Dale and Angle peninsulas, and part of Caldey Island, while a superb limestone section runs from Linney Head to Stackpole Head, with further sections at Lydstep and Giltar Point at Penally. A significant coal measure runs across the county from Saundersfoot to St Brides Bay. After the depositions of the coal measures the land was again subject to massive earth movements, this time the Armorican orogeny of 290 million years ago. However now a WNW-ESE grain was imposed across the south of the county.

The present flatness of the land is due to constant wave erosion at a time when the sea covered the landscape, probably during the late Tertiary period some 17,000 million years ago. Only the more resistant igneous outcrops, like Carn Llidi and Garn Fawr, remained as islands above the sea. On at least 2 occasions Pemrokeshire lay under the Irish Sea glacier; the first occasion, some 120,000 years ago, covered the entire county, while the second, 20 to 17,000 years ago, affected only the north. Before the advent of this last ice sheet drove him south Palaeolithic man, Old Stone Age man, had made his appearance, living in caves on Caldey

Island and at Hoyle's Mouth near Penally. 150,000 years ago the climate became gradually warmer, and with the melting of the ice under the glacier deep and narrow gorges, originally formed with the initial retreat of the glacier, were further deepened as the meltwater scythed it's way to the sea. The Gwaun valley is the most impressive example of a meltwater channel in Britain.

With the final melting of the ice and the rise in sea levels 12,000 years ago the existing river valleys of Milford Haven and Solva were drowned by the incoming tides, assuming their present shape, and the forests were gradually submerged to remain exposed at coastal beaches, as at Whitesand Bay and Amroth, at low tides. At the time Mesolithic man appeared in the county, 10,000 years ago, Britain was still connected to Europe, however by 9,000 years ago Britain has assumed it's present status as an island. Mesolithic man continued to live, much as his ancestor Palaeolithic man had done, by hunting and fishing, with perhaps a little primitive farming, and some movement to open settlement in flimsy shelters. Finds of his flint tools have been made at Nab Head near St Brides Haven, Swanlake Bay near Manorbier, and on Caldey Island. Much of the marshy wooded lowlands where he hunted gradually fell under the encroaching sea — perhaps the tales of great floods, lost cities, and the fine towns of Cantref y Gwaelod (*the Low Hundred*) are folk memories of these drowned lands.

Around 3000 BC Mesolithic man was joined by Neolithic people arriving across the sea in simple craft, not unlike present day coracles. With them they brought the arts of agriculture — how to raise crops and herd animals. It was the Neolithic peoples who began the clearance of the native oak forest, living in flimsy houses, which, but for a single trace at Clegyr Boia near St David's, have disappeared. More enduring, comprising part of Europe's first architecture, are the great stone barrows, the cromlechau or collective burial chambers he left scattered throughout the county. Pentre Ifan near Nevern is one of the finest in Britain, with others, plentiful along the north coast and on the Preselis, rarer in the south. One theory has it that it was Neolithic man who transported the fabled bluestones from Carn Menyn in the Preselis to their present site at Stonehenge.

Circa 1800 BC marked the arrival of the Beaker people from the Low Countries and the Rhine — the name derives from the decorated pottery drinking vessels characteristic of the culture. They favoured individual burial beneath round barrows; Foel Drygarn in the Preselis is the finest example of this type. It was however the introduction of metal tools and weapons and the skills of metal working that transformed the old Mesolithic/Neolithic cultures into the Bronze Age. Stonehenge, in the wider context of Britain, was completed by the early Bronze Age, and is the crowning glory of this culture.

By 550 BC new settlers began to arrive from Gaul, workers in iron, whose traditional heartlands lay in central Europe. These were the Celts, ancestors of the Welsh and Irish. In complete contrast to the Neolithic and Bronze Ages, burial sites disappear from the landscape, to be replaced by easily identifiable hill forts and protected settlements. At St David's Head is one of the finest Iron Age sites, with stone hut circles, defensive walls and ditches and fields, all easily traceable. There are superb hill forts at Foel Drygarn, superimposed on the Bronze Age burial site, and at Carn Ingli; indeed any prominent feature or coastal promontory was seen as a possible settlement site by these warlike tribal people. It is probable that, before modern agriculture obliterated most of their traces, Iron Age settlements were as numerous in the landscape as present day farms. Castell Henllys, near Nevern, is a superb re-creation of an Iron Age settlement. The Roman occupation of 43-410 AD left Pembrokeshire and it's Celtic culture largely unmolested — there is a possible Roman villa site near Amroth, but other traces are very rare.

The 5th and 6th centuries saw a revitalisation of the Celtic culture, based on the new religion of Christianity and the lands around the Irish Sea. This was the Age of the Saints, when St David established his monastic settlement at St David's and St Patrick set out to convert Ireland. The movement was largely monastic, each monastery self-governing, with it's own rules and discipline. With it came a new mysticism and asceticism, something that seemed to suit the Celtic soul. Ascetics chose solitary places to reside, often living in clochàn — beehive shaped buildings made of local stone. There is at Pwll Deri, in Tal y Gaer farmyard, a building which may well have been a clochàn of this type. Pembrokeshire's coast is dotted with beaches and coves where the Celtic saints, the 'peregrini', landed and set sail for Ireland and beyond, and where the solitary could retire for meditation — St Govan's near Bosherston, with it's chapel in a cleft of rock, is the best known of these. Throughout the 9th and 11th centuries the coast was much troubled by Viking raiders, opportunists and adventurers, who gave their own names to many of the more prominent landmarks — Grassholm, Skokholm and Solva all have Norse connections. During this time St David's was burnt no less than 8 times. Truly trial by fire!

The Age of the Saints was also the heroic age of Britain, the age of Arthur, defender of civilisation after the Roman collapse to barbarism. The 11th and 12th century Welsh tales of the Mabinogion relate some of the earliest tales of Arthur in literature; Culwch and Olwen telling of Arthur and his knights' hunt of a magic boar across St David's peninsula, the Nyfer valley and the Preseli hills. However by the late 11th century a new master was in the land. At the time of the Norman invasion Pembrokeshire was part of the kingdom of Deheubarth, modern day Dyfed and the Gower. On the death of Deheubarth's ruler, Rhys ap Tewdwr, in 1093, the doors were open for Norman opportunists and adventurers. Moving from his base on the Severn, Roger, Earl of Shrewsbury, crossed into Pembrokeshire by way of Cardiganshire, his son establishing the Lordship of Pembroke.

The Normans never had sufficient power to retain the whole of

Pembrokeshire, yet the failure of the Welsh to take Pembroke meant that the south of the county became detached from the north, with isolated Norman settlements in the north at Newport and Cilgerran. The new colony was nothing if not fragmented, with land parcelled out among incoming Norman adventurers, who established their forts and castles on the strategic high ground, most with access to river and sea. For a time a definable frontier stretched across the centre of the county from Roch Castle in the west to Amroth Castle on Carmarthen Bay — a frontier termed the Landsker by later historians. South Pembrokeshire formed part of the Marches of Wales, a region where taxes and law were the prerogatives of the Lords in the castle. The new colony was organised on the English pattern, the first such in Wales, and had, by at least 1138, independent 'palatine' status. This is the basis of Pembrokeshire's claim to be the premier county of Wales. Prior to the Norman arrival villages had been the largest settlements; with colonisation came the development of the Anglo-Norman towns, with Pembroke the first county town west of the Severn. The creation of 'Little England beyond Wales' was underway. The local population was absorbed into the growing Norman colony, supplemented by English, Irish and Flemish settlers. To the north, the Welsh maintained their way of life, and their own language — it was not until 1282 that, with the death of Llywelyn the Great, the independence of Wales, of which Deheubarth comprised a part, was finally ended during the Edwardian conquest. From then until the Tudor kings Wales was administered by Welsh and Anglo-Norman nobles, with the Marches as a buffer zone between Wales and England.

Along with Norman adventurism and militarism, often brutal, went great piety. William the Conqueror paid his respects at St David's in 1081. At no time was St David's ever garrisoned, though with growing Norman power an episcopal system was imposed, and, circa 1182, work began on a new cathedral. The Age of the Saints provided plenty of legends and holy sites for the growing number of pilgrims to St David's; hospitals were built for them by Norman bishops at Llawhaden and Whitewell at St David's, there were sisters' houses at Minwear on the eastern Cleddau, and possibly at Angle. Abbeys, priories and chapels were built, as at St Dogmaels, Haverfordwest and St Non's. The Knights Hospitallers of St John of Jerusalem had their Welsh headquarters at Slebech, on the opposite side of the river to Minwear, where they administered to the sick and recruited for the Crusades. Yet for all their piety there was a dark side to the Norman vision. The Celtic vision had been one of nature mysticism and humanity, the Normans introduced savage visions of heaven and hell.

The power of the Norman Lords and their independence was ended with the Act of Union of England and Wales in 1536. Pembrokeshire was made a county, with, for the first time, much the same boundaries as now, and the dissolution of the monasteries ended the power of the abbeys. Pilgrimages were now seen as idolaterous. A new faith was in the land, and all power was under the control of the king, Henry VIII. In the centuries that followed life came to be dominated by the demands of agriculture and trade. Those towns that had access to the sea grew into flourishing ports, and every small creek and cove seemed to have it's own sloop, often locally built. Out went wool, cattle and grain, and in came general merchandise, wine and spices, not to mention the often highly profitable smuggled cargo! The Civil War of the mid 17th century raised tensions and politics between neighbours — the Welsh mainly favoured the king, while the south were, usually, for Parliament — but if politics were uncertain and allegiances inconstant the underlying economy remained stable.

The 19th century had as profound effect on Pembrokeshire as had the arrival of the Normans. The coming of the railways in mid and late century heralded new communication and commercial advantages. Visitors began to arrive in increasing numbers at resort towns such as Tenby and Manorbier, already growing in importance during the late 18th century. 3 new towns were established on the shores around Milford Haven. Neyland, previously a small fishing village, was planned by Brunel as the terminus of his South Wales Railway, and as the terminus of Irish and transatlantic steamships — the latter functions transferring to

18

Fishguard in the late 1900s. Milford Haven was laid out as a private initiative in 1793; among the earliest settlers a group of Quaker whalers from Nantucket, U.S.A. By 1900 to 1914 the town had risen to become one of the busiest fishing ports in the country. Across the water Pembroke Dock grew with the Admiralty dockyard established there in 1814 — for much of the century it was the world's most advanced shipyard, with revolutionary warships and 5 royal yachts to it's credit.

There were many local industrial concerns. Coal mining had always been of importance, production reaching it's peak during the late 18th and early 19th centuries at sites on St Brides Bay, at the confluence of the eastern and western Cleddau, and in the Saundersfoot and Kilgetty area. To exploit the latter's many pits the Saundersfoot Railway and Harbour Company was formed in 1829, and nearby, in Pleasant Valley, the Stepaside Ironworks flourished from 1849 to 1877. Whole villages were given over to quarrying, as at Cilgerran, and at Porthgain and Abereiddi where slates and bricks were also produced. Many of these concerns were comparatively shortlived, and had ceased operating by early or mid 20th century; Hook, on the western Cleddau, was the last colliery, closing in 1949, Porthgain's industrial age ended in 1931, and the Saundersfoot Railway and Harbour Company rail lines were raised by the 1940s. There were changes in agriculture too, cheap fertilizers raised yields and meant the end of the centuries old lime burning industry; cheap imported grain milled in larger town mills meant the end of local flour and feed producing mills; and cheap metals spelt the end of the local smithy. The revolution in land transport meant the end of the coastal trade, and local shipbuilding.

Politically the introduction of county councils in the late 1880s, with elected officials, replaced the centuries rule by the squierarchy, the local landowners who on a voluntary basis had occupied the leading positions in the county. The 19th century was also the hey-day of non conformism, active since the 17th century. Chapels, built out of subscriptions raised by local congregations, began to appear in ever increasing numbers in the towns and villages, particularly in the Welsh speaking areas. Indeed as public buildings the chapels are more truly the Welsh vernacular architecture than the great Norman castles. It was also the age of the restoration of the existing Norman and Celtic churches. Since the Reformation there had been little new church building, and existing churches had been either barely maintained or allowed to decay. Old ones were renovated, and new ones, with inventive variations on existing styles, were built, as at Capel Colman in the north east of the county near Boncath.

By the mid 20th century modernisation had transformed the county. 1960 saw the first oil port, Esso, established. The energy industry, agriculture and tourism, the public services and the small business sector are now the backbones of the local economy. Pembrokeshire was designated Britain's first coastal National Park in 1952, and the long distance Coast Path was opened in 1970. Pembrokeshire returned as a county in it's own right in April 1996, having been from 1974 part of the larger county of Dyfed (Pembrokeshire, Carmarthenshire, Cardiganshire) — the National Park was similarly made a separate authority.

The Country Code

Enjoy the countryside and respect it's life and work.
Guard against all risk of fire.
Fasten all gates.
Keep your dogs under close control.
Keep to the public paths across farmland.
Use gates and stiles to cross fences, hedges and walls.
Leave livestock, crops and machinery alone.
Take your litter home.
Help to keep all water clean.
Protect wildlife, plants and trees.
Take special care on country roads.
Make no unnecessary noise.

Welsh Place Names

Place names can be a fascinating study in their own right, indicating geographical features, patterns of former land ownership, forgotten buildings or former trades. However, the current place name may be far removed from the original name, particularly where there is an anglicised form of an old Welsh name e.g Pembroke is derived from Pen Fro, the Welsh for Land's End. Welsh place names are particularly expressive of geography, and can be highly poetic e.g. Pwll Deri, *pool of the oak trees*. Some of the more common names are listed below:

Aber — river mouth, estuary
Afon — river
Allt — wood, hill, slope
Bach/Fach — little
Bedd — grave
Bryn — hill
Bwlch — pass
Caer(au) — fort(s)
Canol — middle, centre
Capel — chapel
Carn — cairn
Carreg, pl. cerrig — rock, stone
Castell — castle
Cemais — river bend
Cleddau — sword
Coch — red
Coed — wood
Coetan — quoit
Cors — bog, marsh
Craig — rock, cliff
Crib — ridge
Croes — cross
Cromlech(au) — burial mound(s)
Cwm — valley
Cwrw — beer

Cyhoeddus — public
Dan — under
Dau — two
Deri — oak
Dinas — hill fort
Dôl — meadow
Du, Ddu — black
Dŵr — water
Dyffryn — valley
Efail — smithy
Eglwys — church
Ffordd — road
Ffos — ditch, dyke
Ffynnon — spring, well
Gain — fair, fine, elegant
Garn — cairn
Gelli — grove
Glan — river bank
Gors — bog, marsh
Gwastad — level, flat
Gwaun — moor, meadow
Gwyn — white
Gwynt — wind
Hafod — summer dwelling
Hen — old

Hendre — winter dwelling	*Parc* — field, park
Isaf — lower	*Pen* — head, top
Llan — church	*Penrhyn* — promontory, headland
Llannerch — clearing, glade	*Pentre* — village
Llyn — lake	*Plas* — hall
Llwybr — path/track	*Pont* — bridge
Llwyd — grey	*Porth* — harbour
Maen — rock/stone	*Pwll*— pool
Maes — field	*Rhiw* — hill
Mawr/Fawr — great, big	*Rhos* — moorland
Melin — mill	*Rhyd* — ford
Melyn — yellow	*Sych* — dry
Moel/Foel — bare topped hill	*Tafarn* — inn
Morfa — marsh	*Traeth*— beach
Mynach — monk	*Tref* — town, hamlet
Mynachlog — monastery	*Tŷ* — house
Mynydd — mountain	*Uchaf* — upper
Nant — brook, stream	*Y, Yr* — the
Newydd — new	*Yn* — in
Nos — night	*Ynys* — island
Ogof — cave	*Ysgol*— school

A few notes on pronunciation may help:

c — k (hard)
ch — as in lo*ch*
dd — th as in *th*at
f — v
ff — f
g — g (hard)
ll — pronounce l, keep tongue in position at roof of mouth, and hiss!
the — th as in *th*ink

There are 7 vowels, a,e,i,o,u,w and y. Pronunciation may be long or short.

w may be as in pool, or pull e.g. *cwm* (coom) — valley
y may be as in fun, or pin e.g. *y*, *yr* (u, ur) — the, *dyffryn* (dufrin) —
valley

Many Welsh words change their pronunciation and spelling under
certain circumstances e.g. the initial consonant of many words may
soften: b to f, c to g, m to f, p to b etc. Common examples of
mutations are *bach* (little) to *fach*; *mawr* (big) to *fawr*, *porth*
(harbour) to *borth*. Such mutations can make tracing words
through a dictionary a little problematic for the unitiated!

Quick Reference Guide:

For those who have a particular interest in one type of walk e.g.
woodland walks, or in a particular subject e.g. Neolithic burial
chambers, or Bronze Age standing stones and hill forts, the
following quick reference guide is given. The list is not exhaustive,
and only the principal types, or sites, are indicated.

Coastal Walks: 1,2,8-14.
Beaches: good sandy beaches suitable for swimming feature   on
Walks 8: 10-14.
Hill Walks: 4-6,9.
Riverside Walks: 3,5-7.
Woodland Walks: 3,5-7,10.

Stone Age i.e. Palaeolithic, Mesolithic and Neolithic sites:
    2,4,10,12-14.
Bronze and Iron Age sites: 4-6,9,12.
Age of the Saints: 6,7,9,12,13.
Normans: 3,7,12,14 Castles feature on Walk 3 (Cilgerran).
Industrial Heritage sites e.g. mills, mining, shipbuilding,
    quarries: 3,11,13,14.

Information Centres * (Open all year)

Tourist Information Centres:

Cardigan, Theatre Mwldan *	01239 613230
Fishguard, 4 Hamilton Street *	01348 873484
Fishguard Harbour *	01348 872037
Haverfordwest, The Old Bridge *	01437 763110
Milford Haven, 94 Charles Street	01646 690866
Narberth, Town Hall, Market Street *	01834 860061
Pembroke, Commons Road *	01646 622388
Pembroke Dock, Guntower, Front Street	01646 622246
St David's, City Hall, High Street	01437 720392
Saundersfoot, Harbour Car Park	01834 813672
Tenby, The Croft *	01834 842404

Weather Services

Weathercall: Pembrokeshire, Carmarthenshire, Cardiganshire and Powys	0891 500414
Marinecall: Wales	0891 505360
Pembrokeshire County Council (seasonal)	01834 812516

More Walks

The Daugleddau Trail

A circular trail around the Daugleddau estuary above the Cleddau Bridge, via Haverfordwest, Blackpool Mill, Lawrenny, Carew and Llangwm.

Ffos y Mynach (The Monk's Dyke)

A 5 mile/8 kilometre walk across St David's peninsula, from Pen Beri in the north to Ogof y Ffos, near Caer Bwdy Bay, in the south. Leaflet available from Information Centres. Can be combined with the Coast Path to make a circular walk of nearly 20 miles/30 kilometres.

The Golden Road

A long distance route from Crymych across the Preseli hills to Foel Eryri. Can be easily extended by following Gwaun valley footpaths down to Fishguard.

The Knights' Way

A 9 mile/14.5 kilometre path from Blackpool Mill on the eastern Cleddau to Amroth on Carmarthen Bay, via Templeton and Colby Lodge. Leaflet available from Information Centres. The walk is highlighted on the 1:25 000 Outdoor Leisure map for South Pembrokeshire. Provides a link between the Daugleddau Trail and the Coast Path.

The Landsker Borderlands Trail

A 60 mile/95 kilometre circular walk taking in south eastern Pembrokeshire and western Carmarthenshire, with Narberth at it's centre. Leaflet/booklet available from Information Centres. The walk is highlighted on the 1:25 000 Outdoor Leisure map for South Pembrokeshire.

Llysyfran Reservoir and Country Park

There is a fine 7.5 miles/12 kilometres walk around the reservoir. The reservoir is particularly popular with the fishing fraternity — notable especially for it's trout.

The Pembrokeshire Coast Path

One of the national long distance trails. Starts in St Dogmaels near Cardigan, ending at Amroth on the Carmarthenshire border. 186 miles/300 kilometres officially, but in reality nearer 200 miles/320 kilometres.

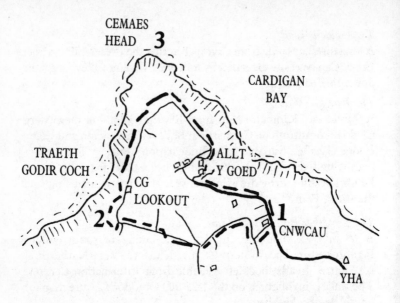

Walk 1   **2.5 miles/4 kilometres**

Cnwcau — Traeth Godir Coch
— Cemaes Head — Allt y Goed — Cnwcau

OS Maps: 1:50 000 Cardigan 145; 1:25 000 Outdoor Leisure 35 North Pembrokeshire/Cardigan (Aberteifi) & Dinas Head 1010 (SN 04/14).

Start: The bridleway adjacent to Cnwcau.

Access: The walk is 1 mile/1.5 kilometres from Poppit Sands, which can be reached on the B4546 from St Dogmaels and Cardigan, or on the minor road from Moylegrove. Bus 407 operates from Cardigan to Poppit Sands summer only.

Parking: Car park in field adjacent to Cnwcau — honesty box.

Grade: Easy — mainly coastal and public footpaths.

Points of Interest:

1. Superb views of the Teifi estuary. Cardigan, tucked away safely behind a bend, takes it's Welsh name from the river. Aberteifi means simply mouth of the Teifi — the Teifi itself rises far to the north in mid Cardiganshire. St Dogmaels, start of the Pembrokeshire Coast Path, owes it's name to St Dogmael, the 5th century grandson of the conqueror of Cardiganshire, Prince Ceredig. Ceredigion is the Welsh name of the county of Cardigan. There are the remains of a 12th century French Tironian abbey in St Dogmaels. Close to the site of St Dogmael's original hermitage, it is well worth a visit. Coastal trade used to cross the much feared Cardigan Bar sandbank, below, to deliver coal, timber and limestone downriver to St Dogmaels and Cardigan, outward bound with local wool, corn, butter and Cilgerran slate. Like many small coastal ports in the 18th and 19th centuries St Dogmaels and Cardigan used to build their own ships. Cardigan Island, across the bay, is owned by the Dyfed Wildlife Trust. It's 40 acres are currently grazed by a rare breed of Soay sheep. Trips to the island only with the permission of the Trust. At one time puffins used to nest on the island, but rats escaped from a wreck nearby and killed them all. There have been recent attempts to get them to return, and cardboard puffins were sited at strategic points. However the real puffins have kept well away. So much for virtual reality!

2. The building to the right of the Coast Path, now falling into disrepair, is a former Coastguard lookout station. The cliffs of this northern section of the coast are the highest in Pembrokeshire, ranging from 400ft/120m to close on 600ft/180m. There is clear evidence of spectacular and ancient faulting and folding in the exposed cliff face as you approach Cemaes Head. Views south to Dinas Island and Strumble Head. Traeth Godir Coch roughly translates as the steep red beach, and may possibly take it's name from the bracken slope above. Brown in winter, it takes on a reddish tint towards sunset.

3. Cemaes Head, Pembrokeshire's most northerly point, takes it's name from the Welsh word cemais i.e. river bend. Maintained as a nature reserve by the Dyfed Wildlife Trust regular cutting of the

bracken allows for open grazing by sheep and rabbit. Gorse, ling, heather and the ubiquitous thrift add variety to the headland's flora. Good hunting territory for choughs, kestrels and peregrine falcon. Given good clear weather views north across Cardigan Bay to Bardsey Island and the Llŷn Peninsula.

4. Cardigan Bay, created by the ocean's eating away of Mid Wales' soft sedimentary rock, is one of the largest bays in Britain, yet much of it is less than 80ft/25m deep. The bay is notable for it's marine mammal population of seals, dolphins and porpoises. There are believed to be an estimated 5,000 seals inhabiting the area from Caldey Island to Aberystwyth, and well over 200 secluded breeding sites. The pupping season extends from September to December, with pups reaching weaning and independence at 3 to 4 weeks. Cardigan Bay is also an important area for the bottlenose dolphins, indeed the bay may be home to one of Britain's last resident populations. More numerous than the dolphins are the harbour porpoises. Swimming low in the water the porpoise requires calm water for identification, unlike the more exuberant dolphins! Visitors to the bay include Orca, or Killer whales, usually August travellers, Minke whales, and the common dolphin, the latter often seen in the company of those master divers, the gannets. The importance of marine life to the bay led, in 1993, to the designation of the area from New Quay south to Tresaith, and out to sea 1 mile from the high water mark, as the Ceredigion Marine Heritage Coast, the first such designation in Britain. The bay has recently been the scene of gas and oil exploration. Inevitably there is the consequent danger of mishap to the resident marine mammal and bird population from pollution, disturbance, or accident.

Walk Directions: [-] denotes Point of Interest

1. From the car park adjacent to Cnwcau [1] turn right onto the road, and again turn right onto the bridleway/green lane just past Cnwcau. Signpost marked 'Bridleway'.

2. Follow the green lane as it bears right and then left. Do not be

tempted by any stiles leading off to the right or left, instead continue to meet a farm gate giving access to a field.

3. Bear right, leaving the bridleway, and continue on another green lane to meet a stile. Cross the stile and bear right over another stile, and bear left on a fenced path.

4. Continue on the path to a stile. Cross this stile, and then immediately cross another stile left to join the Coast Path above Traeth Godir Coch [2].

5. Bear right, and follow the Coast Path to Cemaes Head [3], and continue around right, leaving Cardigan Bay [4] to head inland to Allt y Goed.

6. Go through Allt y Goed farmyard, and follow the road uphill and back to the car park and starting point.

Facilities:

Seasonal parking also possible at Allt y Goed.

Camping at car park by Cnwcau, and at Allt y Goed. Youth hostel nearby. Nearest other facilities are at Poppit Sands, which has a shop/café and a Royal National Lifeboat Institution (RNLI) shop (open 7 days a week in season, in winter weekends only). Also public toilets, BT telephone. Lifeboat and seasonal lifeguard on site. Anyone interested in dolphin, porpoise and bird watching should note that New Quay, north of Cardigan, operate a number of wildlife cruises.

CEIBWR
BAY

1

CASTELL
TRERUFFYDD 2

THE
WITCHES
CAULDRON

4
MOYLEGROVE

TRERIFFITH

3

Walk 2   *4.25 miles/6.75 kilometres*

Ceibwr Bay - The Witches Cauldron
- Treriffith - Moylegrove - Ceibwr Bay

OS Maps: 1:50 000 Cardigan 145; 1:25 000 Outdoor Leisure 35
              North Pembrokeshire/Cardigan (Aberteifi) & Dinas
              Head 1010 (SN 04/14).

Start: Coast Path at Ceibwr Bay.

Access: Ceibwr Bay is 1 mile/1.5 kilometres from
              Moylegrove. Moylegrove can be reached from the
              B4582 Nevern road, or on minor roads from St

Dogmaels and Poppit Sands. Bus 409 from Cardigan to Moylegrove, Tuesdays only!

Parking: Ceibwr Bay.

Grade: Moderate — coastal and public footpaths, some road walking. Steep section at the Witches Cauldron.

Points of Interest:

1. Once the harbour for Moylegrove and the surrounding farmland culm and limestone would have been landed here for turning into the lime required for mortar and sweetening the land. Probably also the odd illicit cargo of wine, tobacco and spices found it's way inland — a little smuggling was a popular activity in 17th and 18th century Pembrokeshire! Indeed one local vicar sadly lamented in 1807 over the amount of Cherbourg cognac that was unerringly finding it's way to Ceibwr! There is an old limekiln by the clapper footbridge over the stream. The bridge itself is recent, and was built following the widening of the stream and destruction of the former concrete and stone bridge by flash floods in 1993. The slate slabs are an import from Snowdonia, but the buttresses are local limestone. Great views from the coast of the dramatic folding and faulting of the northern cliffs. The faulting of the rocks at Pen yr Afr is spectacular. The soft grits and shales of the Ordovician have been twisted by earth movements which occurred in North Western Europe during the Caledonian period at the end of the lower Palaeozoic, some 400 million years ago. The cliffs play host to fulmars, with the local gulls, oystercatchers, cormorants and shags for company, and with the seals for audience.

2. The Witches Cauldron — Pwll y Wrach — is a collapsed blowhole set into the side of a steep valley. The cauldron is connected to the sea via a short tunnel. In a gale, and with a high tide running, a truly dangerous place! On the opposite side of the valley is the Iron Age fort of Castell Treruffydd. It's once near impregnable defensive banks are now falling victim to erosion.

3. Superb views of Pen yr Afr, the coast and the local farmland.

Farming here is mainly devoted to dairying and livestock, with some crop production. The many telegraph posts are much favoured as perches by the buzzards, constantly attentive to the least movement, as is the occasional hovering kestrel. If you are interested in the great stone Neolithic burial chambers, Llech Y Drybedd, out of Pembrokeshire's finest, and set against one of the most stunning views of the Preseli range in the county, lies half a mile/0.75 kilometres away. Turn right and follow the main road away from Moylegrove the short distance to the entrance to Penlan (on the left) and follow the farm track to the field containing the cromlech. The stone is aligned to both the summer and winter solstice sunsets (June 21 and December 22), the sun's rays shining directly into the inner chamber.

4. The pretty village of Moylegrove is set around the bridge over the Ceibwr stream. It has for a backdrop a classic feature of the Pembrokeshire landscape; steep valley slopes and hillsides of bracken and gorse, set with blackthorn and hawthorn. Moylegrove takes it's name from Matilda, wife of Robert Fitz Martin, the first Norman Lord of Cemaes (d.1159). From Grava Matilda in 1291 the village had become Molde Grove by 1326. It was Robert Fitz Martin who founded nearby St Dogmael's Abbey, probably in 1118, endowing it locally with land at St Dogmaels and at Mynachlog Ddu in the Preseli hills. Matilda gave land at Moylegrove — the church was once part of the abbey's holdings. There are 2 chapels in the village, the oldest, Bethel, dates from 1691, whilst Tabernacl, adjacent to the river, a comparative youngster from 1894. The Welsh name for the village, Trewyddel, can be translated as the settlement of an Irishman.

Walk Directions: [-] denotes Point of Interest

1. From the parking bay at Ceibwr Bay [1] walk uphill and turn right to join the coastal path at a wooden stile. Sign here indicating 'Coast Path'.

2. Follow the Coast Path around to the Witches Cauldron [2].

3. From the Witches Cauldron climb the opposite slope to meet a

stile at the top of the rise opposite Castell Treruffydd.

4. Do not cross the stile, instead turn left onto a footpath leading inland, passing between 2 stone pillars which no doubt once served as gate posts — note what were probably the old bolt holes! Post here marked Treriffith, with direction arrow.

5. Continue on the path through woodland to meet a stile giving access to a farm track. Bear left and continue on the track/green lane as it bears right, and then uphill to a farm gate.

6. Turn right and cross a stile into a farmyard, and continue on the farm lane to turn left just past the buildings.

7. Continue on the track up to the main road [3].

8. Turn left onto the road and follow it downhill towards Moylegrove [4]. Ignore the first 2 turnings left to Ceibwr Bay, instead turn left at the minor road by Bethel chapel.

9. Follow the road as it accompanies the stream down to Ceibwr Bay and the starting point.

Facilties:

      Parking also possible in Moylegrove car park.

      BT telephone and public toilets in Moylegrove.

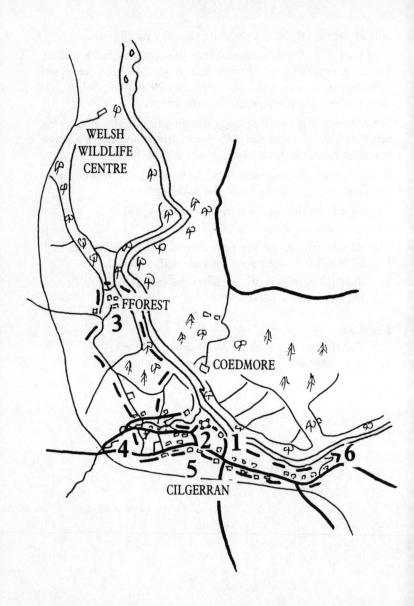

WELSH
WILDLIFE
CENTRE

FFOREST

3

COEDMORE

4

2

1

5

6

CILGERRAN

34

Cilgerran Coracle Centre - Cilgerran Castle - Fforest - Cilgerran Church and Village - Cnwcau - Cilgerran Coracle Centre

OS Maps: 1:50 000 Cardigan 145; 1:25 000 Outdoor Leisure 35 North Pembrokeshire/Cardigan (Aberteifi) & Dinas Head 1010 (SN 04/14), Newcastle Emlyn 1011 (SN 24/34).

Start: Cilgerran Coracle Centre.

Access: Cilgerran is easily reached from the A478 Cardigan to Crymych road. Bus 430 stops at Cilgerran, en route from Cardigan to Crymych.

Parking: Cilgerran Coracle Centre — follow the road down to the river from Cilgerran's main street.

Grade: Easy — woodland, river and farm paths, road.

Points of Interest:
1. Cilgerran gorge, the longest of the Teifi river gorges, is just over 3 miles/5 kilometres long, and owes it's splendid deep isolation to cutting of the rocks during the Ice Age. The original course lay to the west, along the bed of the present tiny river Piliau. The great Irish Sea glacier is believed to have blocked the original course, leaving the Teifi to cut anew. Downriver, at Cardigan, the estuary has formed an extensive saltmarsh. The building of the 'Cardi Bach' railway in 1885, from Cardigan to Whitland, had the effect of dividing the saltmarsh in 2; the result being a freshwater marsh to one side, and a saltmarsh on the other. The railway itself closed in 1963. The Dyfed Wildlife Trust has established the Welsh Wildlife Centre there, noting the area as 'without doubt one of the finest wetland reserves in the Principality . . . " Well worth the visit for the variety of habitats and wildlife on display — the otter is a frequent visitor at least!

The river is tidal to just below Cilgerran, and is home to not just the otter but also sea trout, sewin and salmon, the salmon returning to spawn in the creeks where they were born. The salmon do not always travel alone, for seals follow, and have been seen as far as Cenarth falls, 12.5 miles/20 kilometres from the sea. That other predator, man, has made a living here, fishing from coracles made from local willow, hazel and ash, with skins of hide or calico. The technique is to stretch a net between 2 coracles — the net being held by hand. At one time a net across the river was connected to a bell at Coedmor, the mansion above the river. Medieval Cilgerran had a salmon weir below the castle, with 6 traps, and was rated the finest weir in Wales. A later salmon and sewin weir, below Llechryd's fine stone bridge 2 miles/3 kilometres upstream, was smashed by Rebecca rioters in 1843 in protest at turnpike tolls and interference with local fishermen's livelihood!

2. In an agreement between William I, a visitor to St David's in 1081, and Rhys ap Tewdwr, ruler of Deheubarth (present day Dyfed and the Gower), it was agreed that for £40 a year Rhys could continue to rule Southern Wales. However with the death of William in 1087, and Rhys in 1093, it was open day. Earl Roger of Shrewsbury marched as far as Cardigan, where he built a castle, before moving south where his son established the lordship of Pembroke. Pembroke Castle was eventually given to Gerald of Windsor in 1102, and it was he who crossed the Preselis to establish Cenarth Bychan on what is probably the site of the present castle. Ownership of the castle then passed to alternate attacking Welsh and Normans before a more permanent Norman castle was built by William Marshal the younger in 1223. To William's original drum tower a second was added some years later, which together with strong defensive walls, made it one of the most imposing castles of Wales. Alternatively in disrepair and rebuilt, the castle was by the 18th century a Romantic ruin. Boat trips from Cardigan carried 18th and 19th century tourists and artists upriver to view the castle, perched as bright as the Romantic imagination on it's rocky crag; among the artists Richard Wilson, Peter de Wint and JMW Turner left their impressions.

3. The woodland along this stretch of the Teifi is typical of the wooded slopes of the gorge, with oaks, ash and wild service trees protected from excessive felling by the steepness of the incline. Fforest Farm, a former manor house, was home to Dr Thomas Phaer, physician to Mary I and translator of Virgil's Aeneid. He died in 1560.

4. The church is dedicated to St Llawddog, a 6th century hermit who is believed to have rejected a kingdom — his father was the King of Usk — in favour of a life of contemplation. His example gathered followers, and 6th century churches were dedicated to him here at Cilgerran, and at nearby Cenarth. The present church can be traced back to the 13th century; the tall Norman tower would have acted as a lookout and extra line of defence for those who could not reach the safety of the castle. However the building had fallen into such a poor state of repair by the mid 19th century that in 1855 the whole building, excepting the 13th century tower, was completely rebuilt. There is an ogham stone in the ground, inscribed in Latin and ogham, and dedicated to 'Trenegussus, the son of Macutrenus', who died in the 6th century. Ogham was a script, invented in Ireland by the 5th century, which uses groups of lines to represent Goidelic, the old Irish tongue. Ogham stones are fairly common in Pembrokeshire, and tend to mark the grave of a chieftain. They also provide evidence of strong Irish ties with Pembrokeshire in the 5th to 7th centuries.

5. There may have been a village here, clustered around the 6th century church, but written records date the village from the early 13th century, with the town growing up around the Norman castle. The town became noted for it's great cattle fairs, with 2 summer fairs held by 1800. 1800 was a good year for Cilgerran, a total of 20,000 beasts were sold. Wool was another strong seller, with cargoes taken down to Cardigan from 1600 onwards for sale, particularly to men from North Wales, who wove the wool into suitable clothes for sale in Shrewsbury. With the 19th century slate quarrying came to the fore, and the town took on the aspect of a quarrymen's village. It is now a popular centre for visitors and fishermen.

6. The sharp hairpin slope down to the river served as a ramp to carry slate up from the river quarries to the village above. The Mason's Arms, at the head of the incline, is still known locally as the Ramp Inn. By the 19th century the gorge was littered with slate tips and the quays and towpaths where the barges were loaded with slate for transport downriver to Cardigan. There was even a narrow gauge railway downstream to help trundle away the slate waste. By 1860 5 quarries at least were active, with many quarrymen brought down from North Wales for their expertise, yet by 1891 quarrying had been abandoned. The best slate was exchanged for cargoes of limestone and coal dust (required for mixing with clay to make culm bricks, placed in kilns with the lime to make fertilizer) brought in by ketch from South Pembrokeshire and South Wales. These were cargoes of 'sea slate', suitable for billiard tables, roofing and floors, whilst the poorer 'land slate' were sold locally, often for similar purposes. Some of the local slate was used in restoration work on the church, on village buildings, and as tombstones in the churchyard! In it's heyday the quarry employed some 300 men, which together with the tinplate works at nearby Llechryd, made the area a hive of industrial enterprise. The remains of the slate industry are still here, re-colonised by nature.

Walk Directions: [-] denotes Point of Interest

1. Starting from the Coracle Centre [1] follow the directions for 'Castle and Village' — there is a path left just past the Centre leading up via steps. The 'Riverside Walk' leads to a small slate stone beach below the castle.

2. Once by the castle entrance [2] turn left and then right onto the road leading to the church.

3. Just past 'Ger y Llan' — a residential street on the left, there is a footpath right, indicated by a metal sign of a walking man.

4. Follow the footpath downhill to cross a stream, and continue right, in front of houses, turning left uphill to meet a minor road.

5. Turn left onto the minor road, and passing a house and garage to

your left, turn right over a stile into a field. Signpost here with 'walking man'.

6. Keeping to the right field edge cross to meet a stile giving access to a pine wood.

7. Follow the path as it turns initially right, and then left, as it follows the course of the wooded Teifi gorge. Good views of the river below.

8. Continue through woodland to the stile at Fforest Farm [3]. Cross the farm lane, and continue straight ahead to another stile giving access to a path leading downhill to meet a farm track.

9. Turn right at the farm track and continue downhill to meet an old quarry on the right. Turn sharp left onto a wooded path by the oak tree — signpost here — the footpath leading straight ahead would take you to the main Cardigan road, visible through the trees.

10. Continue on the wooded path to meet the farm track leading to Fforest Farm. Turn right and follow the track down to a tarmac road.

11. At the tarmac road turn left, and then immediately right, descend down stone steps to cross a stream by a concrete footbridge, and then ascend to another tarmac road.

12. Turn left and walk uphill to shortly turn right into Cilgerran Church [4]. Follow the path through the church grounds, and continue on a path to meet the main road through Cilgerran [5].

13. Turn left and follow the road through the village to the Mason's Arms in neighbouring Cnwcau. Immediately adjacent to the pub is a footpath, signposted, leading downhill right, through woodland, then turning sharp left to meet the river [6].

14. Turn left at the river, and follow the track back to the Coracle Centre and the starting point.

Facilities

Parking also possible in Cilgerran village.

All facilities available in Cilgerran. Canoe trips run from the

Coracle Centre — see the river from a different viewpoint!
The Welsh Wildlife Centre, just to the north of the village, is
highly recommended — you may see some of the local otters!

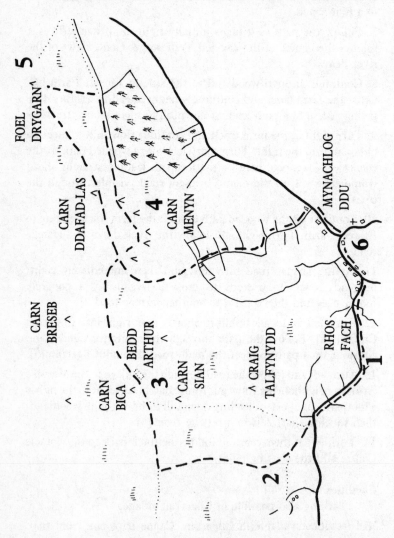

Rhos Fach - Carn Bica - Carn Menyn - Foel Drygarn - Carn Ddafad Las - Mynachlog Ddu - Rhos Fach

OS Maps:	1:50 000 Cardigan 145; 1:25 000 Outdoor Leisure 35 North Pembrokeshire/Newport (Tredraeth) and Eglwyswrw 1033 (SN 03/13).
Start:	Car park at Rhos Fach.
Access:	Rhos Fach is on the outskirts of Mynachlog Ddu, on the minor road leading to the B4313 Maenclochog to Rosebush and Fishguard road. Mynachlog Ddu is 3.5 miles/5.5 kilometres from Crymych. Buses 231 and 430 stop at Crymych, en route from Cardigan.
Parking:	Car park at Rhos Fach.
Grade:	Strenuous - mainly moorland, a little farm track and road walking.

Points of Interest:

1. The most striking feature here is the monument to Waldo, Waldo being Waldo Williams, one of the finest poets in the Welsh language. Born in Haverfordwest in 1904 he was a pacifist and Quaker, an active supporter of Thoreau and Gandhi. His poetry, much influenced by the Romantics, deals with the themes of universal brotherhood and man's relationship with nature. He spent much of his life in this area, reflecting his response in his verse. To give a brief flavour of his work here are 6 lines from 'In Two Fields', in a translation by Tony Conran:

> Where did the sea of light roll from
> Onto Flower Meadow Field and Flower Field?
> After I'd searched for long in the dark land,
> The one that was always, whence did he come?

Who, oh who was the marksman, the sudden enlightener?
The roller of the sea was the field's living hunter.

Opposite is another pillar, more recent, a true bluestone pillar brought down by helicopter in April 1989 from Carn Menyn and set here, whilst it's twin was ferried to Stonehenge to indicate the place of origin of the bluestones of Stonehenge — above and to the north east, at Carn Menyn.

2. The bridleway was one of the major drove routes of northern Pembrokeshire, which led south from Eglwyswrw to Mynachlog Ddu and Maenclochog, utilising the dip in the main ridge between Foel Feddau and Carn Bica. Another major route used the main ridge, droves meeting up in Puncheston for the trek to Crymych. The deeply rutted tracks forged by the cattle are clearly noticeable on the route up to Carn Bica. No turnpike tolls up here to pay! Nowadays the Preseli are common land, grazed by sheep and mountain ponies during the finer weather. There are still traces of the old peat cuttings on Preseli's slopes, which formed such a part of rural life, as it does in parts of Ireland now, well up until the 1920s. Great views on the route up to the main ridge into Craig Y Cwm, and above, Foel Cwmcerwyn, Preseli's highest point, and Foel Feddau. Pembrokeshire's last glacier hid at the bottom of the ridge, some 14,000 years ago. Close to the road are 2 standing stones, Cerrig Meibion Arthur, the Stones of the Sons of Arthur, 2 more victims of the wild boar Twrch Trwyth's wild rampage across the Preselis, hotly pursued by Arthur and his knights.

3. The Preseli as we see them today are the remnants of a mountain chain thrown up during the Caledonian orogeny of 400 million years ago — a mountain range that stretched from Britain to Scandinavia. The high cairns are made of harder igneous rock than the softer surrounding sedimentary and metamorphic rocks. Carn Bica, a typical Preseli cairn, may once have been used as a Bronze Age burial mound, but the stones have been much disturbed over the years. Just below, to the right, is Bedd Arthur, the grave of King Arthur, the small stones delineating a grave of suitable size for so large a hero! At Carn Siân, Jane's Cairn, there is said to have

been a chapel at some time in it's history, though no ruins of it survive. There is a plaque near Carn Sian, unveiled in 1984, in memory of a Liberator which crashed here in September 1944, killing 5 of the 9 man crew. If you are looking for it the grid reference is OS 127322, though it is hard to find!

4. Carn Menyn, or Carn Meini, lays claim to fame as the quarry for the bluestones of Stonehenge. Just how they got to Stonehenge depends very much on what suits the palette. The distance to the monument is 180 miles/300 kilometres and over 80 stones, with a weight of over 250 tons, have been identified as from the Preselis. It has been suggested that the Irish Sea glacier, which at least once in it's history spread as far as Somerset and Avon, transported the stones there in their icy progress, and that when Stonehenge was built these stones were chosen as the most suitable. It was H H Thomas, a geologist, who in the early 1920s discovered that many of the bluestones came from Carn Menyn. He suggested that Neolithic peoples transported the bluestones from one sacred site on the Preselis to another at Stonehenge. In the 1950s the BBC proved that such a feat was possible, using river and land transport. Yet another version has Merlin as the magical agent. However they arrived, the bluestones were eventually, circa 1400 BC, to form the Altar Stone, inner horseshoe, and the middle ring enclosed by the large circle of sarsen stones. There is at Carn Menyn a flat slab, cut as if ready for transport, and known as the altar stone; this may be all that is left of a small burial chamber. No doubt many of the rocks owe their shape to shattering by frost, when the ground was frozen solid during the Ice Age.

5. The Preseli have always been an important area for the peoples of prehistory; it is the dominant landscape feature of northern Pembrokeshire and it's magical grandeur would no doubt have stirred their imagination. Neolithic man scattered his cromlechau, the stone burial chambers, like jewels across Preseli's slopes and at the coast. Pentre Ifan, the most spectacular, lies on it's northern slopes overlooking the Nyfer valley. Bedd Arthur, near Carn Bica, may be the outline of another burial site, whilst the altar stone at Carn Menyn may be the capstone of another. Bronze Age man,

arriving from 1800 BC onwards, found Preseli's cairns ideal as burial mounds, and barrows soon appeared etched against the skyline. Foel Drygarn, the hill of the 3 cairns, is the greatest of these. At the summit are 3 single burial chambers, sited so that they would dominate the landscape. Like Neolithic man, but more frequently, he erected standing stones, occasionally in pairs or rows. They might indicate a waymark, burial site or be a cult object. The stone pillars at Cerrig Meibion Arthur are a fine example, though their exact purpose is not known. Just south of Mynachlog Ddu is the stone circle of Gors Fawr — no Stonhenge, the tallest pillar in the circle is now less than 4 feet/1.25 metres high — but it can still impress. It would have been used for ceremonial purposes. The trackway across the Preselis from Foel Drygarn, sometimes called the Flemings Way, was used as a routeway to Whitesand Bay and the Wicklow Hills in Ireland, where gold for trade was the lure. Iron Age man, arriving from 550 BC, found Preseli's high cairns ideal as defensible hill forts. Double ramparts and ditches were added where necessary to Foel Drygan's slopes. Both hut sites and enclosures are still traceable.

Rebecca

The 1830s and 1840s were turbulent times for European governments. In continental Europe 1848 witnessed not only the great radical social and political revolutions, almost global in their wildfire enthusiasm and spread, but also the publication of the Communist manifesto. In England in the 1830s 'General Ludd', active since 1811, continued to wreck the power looms, while 'Captain Swing' smashed the new threshing machines. The Chartist manifesto and the Chartists of the late 1830s and 1840s demanded and demonstrated for universal suffrage. In Ireland the great famine of 1845 to 1846 resulted in the death of a million by starvation, and the emigration of another million.

In West Wales the small farmers and the people found themselves trapped in poverty, unable to pay the rents and rates, the tolls and taxes, demanded of them. They felt under siege, serfs to an alien squirearchy and magistracy, who spoke a different language and belonged to another class and religion. They turned to the religion they knew, and read in Genesis 24 verse 60 'And they blessed Rebecca, and said unto her, Thou art our sister, be thou the mother of thousands of millions, and let thy seed possess the gate of those which hate thee'.

Particularly resented was the more stringent imposition of tolls at the turnpike gates in 1839, and with the lime carting season beginning — lime being necessary for sweetening the acid soils — matters came to a head at Efailwen, south of Mynachlog Ddu. On 13 May the toll gate was destroyed, and the toll house burnt to the ground. Communal justice in this part of Wales had always been executed in an atmosphere of drama and fiesta — offenders had been mounted on a wooden cocking horse and paraded around — and accordingly at the newly re-erected turnpike gate at Efailwen appeared a mob of 400 to oppose 7 special constables. All were in disguise, many with blackened faces and in women's clothes. The gate was again smashed, and the pattern was repeated elsewhere. Their leader — probably a Thomas Rees, a peasant farmer and fighter from near Mynachlog Ddu — was openly referred to as 'Rebecca'.

After a brief respite in 1840 and 1841 'Rebecca' re-appeared with a vengeance in 1842 and 1843, and West Wales, from Cardiganshire to Pembrokeshire and Carmarthenshire, was virtually ungovernable. Nightly gates were smashed and toll houses burnt down, and the established pattern of posted notices in chapels, the ritual at the gate with Rebecca as an old mother hindered by the gate, consequently to be smashed down by Rebecca and her 'children', together with the beating up of special constables, was continued. The country was policed by marines sent in by Government. A few of Rebecca's Daughters were caught, tried and deported, but with a Government enquiry appointed in 1844, and subsequent legislation revoking many of the grievances, matters improved, and the 1850s witnessed an era of greater prosperity.

★ ★ ★

6. Mynachlog Ddu means simply 'black monastery', and refers to the fact that the Benedictine monks of St Dogmael's Abbey, near Cardigan, had sheep grazing rights here, with hill granges on the Preseli. The Benedictines were famous for their black habit. No monastic buildings were ever built. There is a fine imposing chapel in the village. Built in 1794 Bethel keeps the grave of Thomas Rees, or Twm Carnabwth, *Tom Stonecottage*, said to be the original Rebecca of the Rebecca Riots. It was at his 'tŷ unnos', literally a primitive "one night" cottage erected overnight by the landless on common land, that the rioters gathered for their historic march on Efailwen toll gate.

Walk Directions: **[-] denotes Point of Interest**

1. Starting from Rhos Fach [1] turn left out of the car park onto the minor road. Continue for just over 0.5 miles/0.75 kilometres until the road turns to the left.

2. Turn right onto the open moorland and ascend to the main Preseli ridge by the bridleway [2], which leads off left around the spur above. The route is clearly indicated by a signpost. Alternatively ascend directly up the spur to follow an undefined route to the rocks of Craig Talfynydd and Carn Siân, and then on to Carn Bica. The standing stones of Cerrig Meibion Arthur are close to the road, to the left of the bridleway.

3. Once at the main ridge turn right onto a well defined track and continue towards Carn Bica. The white posts here indicate the route of an annual hill race held to commemorate the Rebecca Riots — the Ras Becca. The white posts will lead you to Carn Bica, but thereafter their route differs.

4. From Carn Bica [3] follow the clearly defined path past Bedd Arthur to Carn Menyn [4], original home of the bluestones of

46

Stonehenge. The path from Carn Bica has a fine backdrop of 6 rock outcrops, marching out from Carn Breseb, guarding it's northern flank.

5. From Carn Menyn and Carn Cyfrwy follow the well defined path as it skirts the forestry plantation. There is a fine dry stone wall sheepfold adjacent to one of the cairns just before the forestry is reached. Directly opposite the end of the forest there is a path left. This will take you directly to the summit of Foel Drygarn [5].

6. From Foel Drygarn descend and make directly for Carn Ddafad-las.

7. Keeping Carn Ddafad-las to your right continue to meet the track used for the ascent of Carn Menyn. Keeping Carn Menyn above you and left, descend left to join a path leading down to farmland.

8. Make for a well defined lane running between stone banks, with sheep pens on the right by the lane entrance. Follow the lane as it descends to meet the road into Mynachlog Ddu [6].

9. Turn right and follow the road through the village. Where the road continues ahead to Maenclochog and Efailwen turn right to return to the starting point.

Facilities:

BT telephone kiosk and Post Office in Mynachlog Ddu. Post Office open Monday to Thursday half days only. No other facilities.

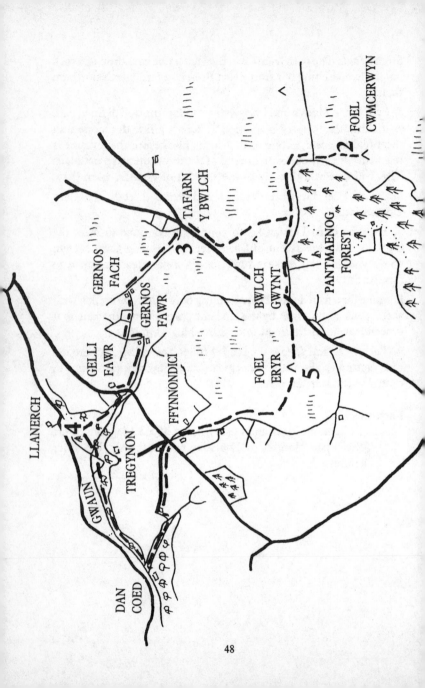

Bwlch Gwynt - Foel Cwmcerwyn (Preseli Top) - Tafarn y Bwlch - Gernos Fawr - Gernos Fach - Gelli Fawr - Gwaun Valley - Dan Coed - Penralltddu - Ty Gwyn - Foel Eryr - Bwlch Gwynt

The walk may be shortened by omitting the 2.5 miles/4 kilometres required for the ascent of Foel Cwmcerwyn from Pantmaenog Forest gate, and/or by omitting the Gwaun valley section of just over 3 miles/5 kilometres.

OS Maps:	1:50 000 Cardigan 145; 1:25 000 Outdoor Leisure 35 North Pembrokeshire/Newport (Tredraeth) and Eglwyswrw 1033 (SN 03/13).
Start:	Car park at Bwlch Gwynt.
Access:	Bwlch Gwynt is on the B4329 mountain road across the Preseli, from Eglwyswrw south to Haverfordwest. It is 1.5 miles/2.5 kilometres from the crossroads with the B4313 Maenclochog to Fishguard road at the New Inn, and 1 mile/1.5 kilometres from Tafarn y Bwlch. No buses.
Parking:	There is a parking area at Bwlch Gwynt.
Grade:	Strenuous — moorland, farm tracks and woodland.

Points of Interest

1. Bwlch Gwynt — the windy pass — stands at the highest point of the mountain road from North to South Pembrokeshire. From here stretches the Golden Road 8 miles/12.75 kilometres across the Preseli hills to the great Bronze Age cairn of Foel Drygarn. Bronze Age man used the trackway as a trade route to Whitesand Bay and Ireland, trading Preseli axes for copper and gold from the Wicklow

hills. The track has had many names — the Pilgrim's Way, the Roman Road, the Robber's Road. It was also known as the Flemings' Way, for the simple reason that Flemish settlers brought into the county by colonising Normans found it safer to take to the 'tops', out of the way of ambushing Welsh. 1,000s of cattle, sheep and pigs, even geese, with their drovers, would have used the route, particularly with the coming of toll gates to the plains. Herds from Ireland and Fishguard gathered at Puncheston for droving up to Bwlch Gwynt, here to meet cattle and sheep from Newport — all destined for markets on the Welsh borders and in England.

2. At 1760 feet/536 metres Foel Cwmcerwyn, or *Preseli Top* as it is known locally, is Pembrokeshire's highest point. Trig point and Bronze Age cairns on the summit. Richard Fenton, Pembrokeshire's historian, came here in 1806 in a party, with fine ladies in crinoline, to excavate the cairns. The urn he found has not survived, but a drawing of it indicates it to have been well decorated, suggestive of continuing contact with Ireland. Good views to the south of Rosebush and Llys y Fran reservoirs — on good days Snowdonia, the Wicklow hills in Ireland, and maybe Devon. There was a small slate quarry below the summit, but it's remoteness made it a short lived concern. The village of Rosebush, tucked away beneath Pantmaenog Forest, enjoyed a brief fame in the 1870s, when a nephew of Lord Macauley developed it as a mountain resort. The railway was extended to the village from Clunderwen in 1876 to carry visitors and export the local quarry's blue slate. However few visitors came, and the quarry ceased operation in 1906. The small hotel built of corrugated iron zinc is now the local pub. The village is well worth a visit!

Of Wild Boars and Kings

In that superb book of medieval Welsh tales, the Mabinogion, the story of Culwch and Olwen relates the royal hunt of Arthur in the chase of the magic boar, Twrch Trwyth. Culwch, in love with Olwen, had requested her hand, but with a giant as prospective father-in-law things were never going to be easy. Ysbaddan Giant required, among other items, the comb and shears from between the ears of Twrch Trwyth with which his 'hair may be dressed, so exceeding stiff it is'. Culwch accordingly enlisted the help of his cousin, Arthur.

The hunt began in Ireland, where Twrch Trwyth, a former king who for his wickedness had been turned into a swine, was laying waste the country. Pursued by Arthur and his knights, Twrch Trwyth crossed to Wales, landing at Porth Clais near St David's. The magic boar then proceeded to slaughter men and cattle on his way across St David's peninsula to Foel Cwmcerwyn in the Preseli. There, on Preseli ridge, many of Arthur's knights were slain, their bodies turning instantly to stone. Cerrigmarchogion, the Knights' Stones, marks the spot.

Twrch Trwyth was finally driven into the Severn estuary and on into Cornwall, where the comb and shears were taken from him. Culwch duly gained his reward. Twrch Trwyth, however, escaped into the sea. So if you see any wild boar on your walks — you have been warned!

★ ★ ★

3. As the name Tafarn y Bwlch suggests, there was once an inn here. Drovers travelling south from the collecting centre of Eglwyswrw would have met drovers and their herds travelling east from the farms around Newport. Many of these drovers' inns would have acted as resting places — on a good day cattle could be driven 20 miles/30 kilometres, pigs only 6 miles/10 kilometres — and there was always the problem of where to spend the night. From Tafarn y Bwlch the drovers would have had a good view of the route across the Preseli. It was the coming of the railways that led to the end of the droves and their unique way of life. Nowadays the Preseli are mainly common grazing land for ponies and sheep — many of the sheep being moved south to Castlemartin peninsula in the winter. The walk follows the route of the main drove trail from Newport, which, after crossing Carningli Common,

descended to Llannerch by way of Pen Rhiw, and then began the ascent to the Preseli via Gelli Fawr, Gernos Fawr and Fach, and Tafarn y Bwlch, finally ascending the track across the moorland to the main ridge by Pantmaenog Forest gate.

4. The Gwaun valley was carved out during the last Ice Age as a meltwater channel. The river itself rises on Foel Eryr's slopes, and begins it's descent to Fishguard by Gernos Fawr. It's slopes are densely wooded with oak, with alder and willow clinging close to the river. The Gwaun valley, along with the Daugleddau, is one of the few remaining areas of semi-natural woodland left in Pembrokeshire, and is an area of rare beauty. The dippers and grey wagtails that frequent the hidden rock pools and the river make a fine contrast with the wild moorland pipits, larks and buzzards. The valley's steep slopes have helped to keep communities and the natural landscape apart from the rest of the county, and preserve local traditions and individuality. When the new Gregorian calendar replaced the Julian calendar in 1752 local tradition ignored it. The Gwaun valley has the distinction of sharing with Lerwick in the Shetland Islands a New Year's Day of January 13!

5. Foel Eryr, *Eagle's Hill*, stands at 1535 feet/468 metres. As at Foel Cwmcerwyn there is a Bronze Age burial cairn at the summit. As with the Preselis as a whole the prevailing vegetation is predominantly open moorland, heath and bog, with heather, gorse, bilberry and the bright yellow tormentil; and in boggy areas, rushes and the white tufts of cotton grass. The bilberry's edible black berries rarely show, however, as they are too close cropped by ponies and sheep for survival. There is a viewing point at the summit, giving place names and orientation.

Walk Directions: [-] denotes Point of Interest

1. Starting from Bwlch Gwynt [1] car park follow the moorland track alongside the fence, and continue ahead, keeping Pantmaenog Forest on your right.

2. Just over .5 miles/.75 kilometres a wooden gate leading right

onto a forest track and down to Rosebush village will be reached —
note the wide track leading left as this will be the route taken down
to Tafarn y Bwlch after the ascent of Foel Cwmcerwyn.

3. Continue ahead, keeping the forest on your right, until a stile
right leading onto open moorland is reached.

4. Cross the stile onto a path which almost immediately bears
diagonally left to gain the rise leading to the summit.

5. Continue to the OS trig point on the summit of Foel Cwmcerwyn
[2].

6. Retrace your steps the 1.25 miles/2 kilometres to the forest gate
noted at paragraph 2, and turn right onto the wide path leading
downhill. This was 1 of the major routes across the Preseli before
the building of the present tarmac road.

7. Continue downhill — keeping to the left of the track is probably
the easier route. Great views directly ahead of the rocks of Carnedd
Meibion Owen, and Carn Ingli to the left. To the right the slopes of
Preseli, as if scooped out by a spoon.

8. At the tarmac road turn right, and continue to Tafarn y Bwlch
[3].

9. Just past the cattle grid and BT telephone box turn left through a
farm gate — sign here indicating 'Bridleway' — and continue on
the farm track to Gernos Fach.

10. Once at the farm of Gernos Fach turn left, walk through the
farmyard, and continue downhill on a farm track/green lane to
enter a field. Cross the 1st field and enter a 2nd field.

11. Continue to the bottom left of this field and turn left onto a
green lane leading down to Gernos Fawr.

12. At Gernos Fawr turn right, walk through the farm, and follow
the farm track downhill for .5 miles/.75 kilometres to a tarmac
road. The streams here, on their way down from the moorland
above, make up the headwaters of the river Gwaun.

13. Turn right and continue to Gelli Fawr. At Gelli Fawr turn left
over a stile — signpost here marked 'Public Footpath' — and
continue towards the bottom right of the field and a stile.

14. Cross the stile and then immediately turn left over another stile and continue downhill on the woodland path into the Gwaun valley [4].

15. At the bottom of the path turn left onto another path. Signpost marked 'Tregynon'. The path right, marked 'Public Footpath', leads to Llanerch and the main tarmac road through the Gwaun valley.

16. After .25 miles/.5 kilometres there is a path leading left and uphill to Tregynon, and so signposted. Continue ahead instead on the woodland path.

17. After nearly a mile/1.5 kilometres cross a stile just before Dan Coed, turn left, and continue uphill. Signpost here, marked, to the left 'Bridleway'. Ahead marked 'Pontfaen'.

18. Continue ahead for .5 miles/.75 kilometres to meet a farm track. Bear left and continue through the farmyard of Penralltddu and onto the tarmac road leading to Ty Gwyn and the minor road from Gelli Fawr.

19. Turn right onto the minor road, passing Ffynnondici on your immediate left, and shortly turn left through the farm gate adjacent to the turning to Berthe Gwynne. Signpost here indicating 'Bridleway'.

20. Follow the track up, initially keeping to the right boundary fence, then head directly up ahead through the bilberries to the summit of Foel Eryr [5].

21. Once at the summit there is pleasant downhill stretch to the car park at Bwlch Gwynt and the starting point.

Facilities:

Parking also possible at Tafarn y Bwlch, on the minor road between Gelli Fawr and Ffynnondici, or in the Gwaun valley near Llannerch, or at Sychbant picnic site.

BT telephone box at Tafarn y Bwlch. Gelli Fawr offers self catering, a coffee shop and bar. There is a country farmhouse hotel and restaurant at Tregynon. Nearest pubs at Pontfaen in the Gwaun valley, or at the New Inn at the crossroads of the Eglwyswrw to Haverfordwest and Maenclochog to Fishguard roads.

CARN INGLI

2 ^ CARN
INGLI

CARNINGLI
COMMON

BEDD
MORRIS

3

CARN
EDWARD

DOLRANNOG

PENLAN
UCHAF

LLANERCH

SYCHBANT
PICNIC SITE

1

GWAUN

Sychbant Picnic Site - Gwaun Valley - Llanerch - Carn Ingli - Carningli Common - Bedd Morris - Sychbant Picnic Site

OS Maps:	1:50 000 Cardigan 145; 1:25 000 Outdoor Leisure 35 North Pembrokeshire/Newport (Trefdraeth) and Eglwyswrw 1033 (SN 03/13)
Start:	Sychbant picnic site
Access:	Sychbant picnic site is situated 1.5 miles/2.5 kilometres from Pontfaen in the Gwaun valley. Pontfaen itself can be reached from the B4313 Fishguard to Maenclochog road, or on the minor road from Dinas or Newport on the north coast. No buses — nearest public transport access point at Newport.
Parking:	Sychbant picnic site.
Grade:	Strenuous — mainly moorland and woodland paths. A little road walking.

Points of Interest:

1. The delightful Gwaun valley — gwaun is Welsh for *moor* — was formed as a sub glacial meltwater channel of the formidable Irish Sea glacier. Rising on the slopes of Foel Eryr the river Gwaun runs for 8.5 miles/14 kilometres down to Lower Fishguard, supplying Fishguard with it's Welsh name in the process; Abergwaun translates as mouth of the river Gwaun. Characteristic of the valley are the steep oak woods which fringe the river as it meanders on it's course past small farms and the occasional isolated settlement. Sychbant's wooded slopes above are deciduous, backed by pine plantation.

2. Once the core of a volcano the views from the present summit of

Carn Ingli are quite superb. To the north are the rocks of Snowdonia, with the full panorama of the Preseli swinging around you to your right, whilst the splendid sea coast of Newport and Fishguard Bays lie etched below. Iron Age settlers built a fort here, one of the best preserved in Britain. The still impressive single defensive wall in it's heyday would have been 6 foot/1.75 metres high by 6 foot/1.75 metres thick. Easily traceable in the landscape are numerous hut circles and enclosures. Probably occupied until late Roman times it would have been home to some 150 people. The later Norman Lord of Cemais, William Martin, fearing a different kind of threat, chose to site his 12th century castle on more sheltered and accessible ground in present day Newport. One later famous Lord of Cemais and owner of Newport Castle was Pembrokeshire's Elizabethan historian George Owen.

One noteable Carn Ingli resident is said to have been the 6th century Irish St Brynach. A friend and contemporary of St David he founded a number of churches in the area, of which the church at Nevern, dating from 570, was the most important. Preferring to live the life of a hermit he chose Carn Ingli's splendid isolation as home. However St Brynach was no ordinary hermit. Not only was his coach driven by stags and his cows herded by a wolf, but he was also ministered to by a flight of angels. Quite possibly Carn Ingli takes it's name from the legend of St Brynach's life, and the Rock or Mount of Angels, Carn Angylion. In recent times stone was quarried from Carn Ingli's steep rock face and transported via a cable railway to a crushing plant on the road below. 2 stone pillar blocks at the head of the incline are all that now remain of this brief industrial intrusion. Carningli Common and Mynydd Caregog are typical of Pembrokeshire's upland scenery; gorse, bilberry and heather predominate, with occasional blocks of pine plantation to break the open horizon. In late summer and autumn the yellows and purples of the gorse and heather turn the landscape into a glorious exhibition of abstract colour.

3. The standing stone here traditionally marks the grave of Morris, or Morus, hence the Welsh name Bedd (grave) Morris. Morris himself was a notorious highwayman who took shelter amongst the

rocks commanding the road down to Newport. Preferring bow and arrow as his method of attack, he trained his dog to retrieve any arrows that failed to meet their target. Incensed at this unseemly behaviour Morris was taken by the local populace, hanged, and buried beneath the stone. The stone itself is probably Bronze Age in origin, and would no doubt have indicated an important trade route. It has served for centuries as a boundary stone to Newport parish, and the word 'Newport' can still be picked out, cut into the stone.

Walk Directions: [-] denotes Point of Interest

1. Starting from Sychbant picnic site turn left onto the minor road running through the Gwaun valley [1] and continue to Llannerch.

2. At Llannerch leave the minor road — there is a sign here marked Bridleway — and cross the farm drive, keeping to the left of the farmhouse, to reach a gate giving access to a farm track.

3. Go straight ahead, uphill, on the farmtrack, until, leaving the oak wood behind, you reach the farm road to Penrhiw Farm.

4. Continue straight ahead on the farm road, passing Dolrannog Uchaf and Dolrannog Isaf, to gain open country. Carn Ingli's splendid features are now left and above [2].

5. Turn left and follow the path leading up to Carn Ingli. Initially the path skirts the stone field walls on the left. There is then the choice to either follow the easier path leading left around Carn Ingli, thus allowing for the ascent to the top to be made from more even ground, or to choose a pleasant scramble up the rocks to reach the summit this way. Either way glorious views are the deserved reward!

6. From Carn Ingli follow the track leading ahead and left to cross Carningli Common to Carn Edward.

7. Carn Edward itself is in a field, and there is a public footpath passing to the left of it. However do not cross the stile, instead continue ahead, keeping the fence on your left.

8. Follow the well defined path across Mynydd Caregog for over 1

mile/1.5 kilometres until the standing stone of Bedd Morris [3] and the minor road between Pontfaen and Newport is reached — there is a small parking area here.

9. Cross the stile, left, adjacent to the farm gate and cattle grid, to enter a field.

10. Turn left and cross the field to the forestry plantation, initially keeping the fence to your immediate left, and then bearing diagonally right after a short distance to reach the stile leading into the wood.

11. Cross the stile and follow the wide path through the pine wood to emerge by an open field protected by a wire fence. You are now back on the Gwaun valley slopes.

12. Continue right, down through the wood, to reach a stile on your left. Ignore this stile as it leads to Ffald y Brenin (marked Sychbant on the OS map) and continue the short distance to a second stile where the path leaves the woodland.

13. Continue downhill on a grassy path, passing a bench on your left, to cross right a small stream by a wooden footbridge.

14. Continue downhill into the valley to reach Sychbant picnic site and the starting point.

Facilities:

Parking is also possible at the foot of Carn Ingli on the side of the road giving access to Dolrannog and Penrhiw farms, and at the small car park at Bedd Morris. Alternatively walk up to Carn Ingli from Newport to join the walk at Point 2.

Picnic site and public toilets at Sychbant. Penlan Uchaf, almost adjacent to Sychbant, offers cream teas and gardens in season. Christian retreat at Ffald y Brenin. Pony trekking at Dolrannog Isaf. Good pub in Pontfaen.

Nevern (Nanhyfer) - Llwyngwair
- Pontnewydd - Pilgrims' Cross
- Nevern (Nanhyfer)

OS Maps:	1:50 000 Cardigan 145; 1:25 000 Outdoor Leisure 35 North Pembrokeshire/Cardigan (Aberteifi) & Dinas Head 1010 (SN 04/14), Newport (Tredraeth) and Eglwyswrw 1033 (SN 03/13)
Start:	Nevern
Access:	Nevern is .5 miles/.75 kilometres north of the A487 Newport to Eglwyswrw road. Bus 412 (Haverfordwest — Fishguard — Newport — Cardigan) will stop at the turning to Nevern.
Parking:	Limited parking in Nevern village, or at the Trewern Arms if you are a patron.
Grade:	Easy — mostly field, green lane and riverside path.

Points of Interest:

1. One of the prettiest villages in Wales Nevern has had a rich and colourful history. St Brynach, to whom the present church is dedicated, established a religious settlement in the 6th century. A native of Ireland he had made his way here after pilgrimage to Rome, followed by sojourn in Brittany. He established a number of churches in the area, but seems to have preferred to live the life of a hermit on Carn Ingli, the 'Rock of Angels'. A friend and contemporary of St David he is believed to have died on 7 April 570, St Brynach's day. A later conqueror, this time of lands not souls, was Robert Fitz Martin, a Norman landowner from Devon, who took the old hundred of Cemais for himself to create a Norman enclave within Welsh territory. He built himself a fine castle at Nevern circa 1100, probably on the site of an earlier Iron Age

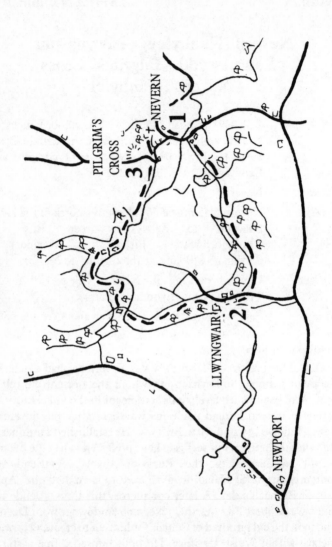

settlement. His grandson William Martin had reason to regret the choice when he was driven out by the Lord Rhys, the native ruler of Deheubarth (Dyfed and the Gower) in 1191. William then built himself a more substantial castle at Newport, possibly dating from 1195.

Before they were driven out of Nevern the Normans had time to build a church on St Bryanch's site, yet all that now remains is the 12th century tower. The rest of the church is late 14th century/early 15th century, and was much restored in 1864. The church and churchyard still, however, hold hidden treasure. Embedded in the window sills of the south chapel, the Trewern-Henllys chapel, are 2 rare stone slabs found in 1906. The Maglocunus stone is a late 5th century memorial stone to Maglocunus, son (fili) of Clutorius. The inscriptions are in both Latin and ogham. Ogham is a script developed in Ireland by the late 5th century and is made up of a series of lines cut across the edge of the stone. Each letter of this Latin based alphabet is named from a tree or plant e.g. *b* from *beith* (birch). Next to it is the fine 10th century Cross Stone. There is another bilingual memorial stone outside by the porch, to the 5th/6th century Welsh chieftain Vitalianus. However the pride of Nevern is the magnificent 10th or 11th century Great Cross — there are other superb examples at Carew and Penally. In former days the cuckoo is said to have sung from the head of the stone on St Brynach's day.

The fine avenue of English yews is believed to be 600 years old — the 2nd yew on the right from the churchyard entrance is famous for the almost continuous blood red sap that drips, some say, for a monk who was wrongly hung from the branches above. The line of Irish yews along the road were planted as a memorial to those who fought in the 1st World War. The mounting block by the entrance is 1 of only 2 left in Pembrokeshire, no doubt the occasional horse rider still makes use of it! The Nevern valley features in the medieval tales of the Mabinogion, for Twrch Trwyth, the wild boar, was pursued through the valley by Arthur and his knights to the Preseli hills. Nowadays the river is hunted for salmon and sewin, returning from the sea at Newport Bay.

2. Llwyngwair Manor, now a hotel and caravan park, has a fine manor house. The country seat of the Bowens from 1540 until the family line recently died out the house has been much altered over the years, and is in effect an amalgam of styles from Tudor to Victorian. The Bowens were great patrons of the Methodists, and William Williams Pantycelyn wrote one of his most popular hymns here. Reflecting it's setting Llwyngwair translates as hay grove. Pontnewydd, (*new bridge*), was built by the Bowens at a suitable crossing over the river Nyfer.

3. Cut into the rock face here is the 2 foot high Pilgrims' Cross, with, below, a natural ledge where pilgrims may have knelt to supplicate the saints. Tradition has credited Nevern with being last stage on the pilgrim route to St David's from St Dogmael's Abbey and North Wales. Certainly there were at one time 8 pilgrim chapels of ease in Nevern parish, although by Elizabethan times they were in ruins. It is possible that this was the site of a healing well, Pistyll Brynach. Holy wells, springs, standing stones and Celtic church sites were much in favour as sources of bodily and/or spiritual strength. To the left of the cross, away from the road, are curious steps in the rock where the path begins a short ascent. No doubt cut by water there is a small graffiti cross cut into the stone. It is unlikely that pilgrims would have continued on the path to Newport, there are more direct routes, but pilgrimages were protracted affairs, with many side trips to different sites, and this would have been a wayside shrine, now almost unique.

Walk Directions: [-] denotes Point of Interest

1. Starting in Nevern [1] take the footpath leading across the field between the Trewern Arms and Nevern bridge — access across a stile next to a metal gate. Signposted Cwm Gwaun and Bedd Morus.

2. Once across the field cross another stile onto a wooded green lane. Continue on the green lane to reach the minor road by Llwyngwair Manor (now a hotel and caravan park) [2] — great views left en route of Carn Ingli's rock peak.

3. Turn right. Continue past the old farm buildings. Where the road continues right to Llwyngwair Home Farm continue ahead on a track, marked Pontnewydd. Signposted 'Public Footpath'.

4. Just past the bridge, and opposite a house on the left, is a footpath leading right and marked Nevern. Continue on this path, past a ruined cottage, to gain the riverside path.

5. Where the path meets a concrete roadway by a private house continue straight ahead across a stone footbridge, cross another private roadway and again go straight ahead, through a metal gate.

6. Turn immediately right, signposted 'Public Footpath', and cross the field to a stile to reach a path high above the river. Continue to reach another field.

7. Go ahead across the field, and keeping to the right field edge, reach a stile at the top right of the field. Cross onto the path leading past the Pilgrims' Cross [3] to reach the road into Nevern.

8. At the road go ahead downhill — the castle site is along the road to the left — and where the road bears right continue ahead on a footpath by the side of a house to reach the church across an attractive stone footbridge.

9. At the church either continue along the footpath by the side of the church wall by a stream, or continue through the churchyard. From the church it is a short distance back to the starting point.

Facilities:

> BT telephone, public toilets (by the community hall) and the Trewern Arms. Accommodation available in the village. Llwyngwair Manor is a popular caravan park. Pentre Ifan, possibly the finest Neolithic burial chamber in Britain, is 2 miles to the south on a minor road; Castell Henllys, a recreation of an Iron Age fort, is 2 miles to the north on the A487. Both are signposted.

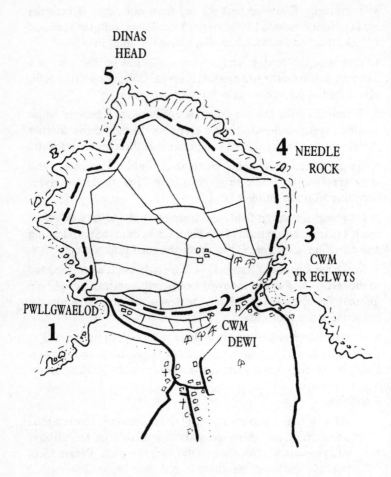

DINAS
HEAD

5

4 NEEDLE
ROCK

3

CWM
YR EGLWYS

PWLLGWAELOD

1

2

CWM
DEWI

Pwllgwaelod - Cwm yr Eglwys
- Dinas Island - Pwllgwaelod

OS Maps: 1:50 000 St David's and Haverfordwest 157, Cardigan 145; 1:25 000 Outdoor Leisure 35 North Pembrokeshire/Cardigan (Aberteifi) & Dinas Head 1010 (SN 04/14), Newport (Trefdraeth) and Eglwyswrw 1033 (SN 03/13).

Start: Pwllgwaelod

Access: Pwllgwaelod can be easily reached from Dinas, which is situated on the A487 Fishguard to Cardigan road. Bus 412 stops at Dinas, en route from Haverfordwest to Cardigan.

Parking: Free parking at Pwllgwaelod.

Grade: Moderate — coastal and valley path.

Points of Interest:

1. Pwllgwaelod, which translates as 'bottom pool', has always been a popular beach, and can get crowded on hot summer days. There was a notable pub here, the Sailor's Safety, which first opened for business in 1593, but it has recently closed it's doors after 400 years of sterling service. A light was displayed after dark to guide sailors across Fishguard Bay to the safety of the shore. The limekiln, a little way inland from the beach, would have produced lime for fertilising Dinas Island Farm, and farms around Dinas village.

2. Cwm Dewi is a pleasant marshy and wooded valley, much appreciated by the local birdlife, and watched over by the Dinas Island rabbits and sheep. It was formed some 17,000 to 20,000 years ago as a meltwater channel for the glacier then blocking Newport Bay, making Dinas Island truly an island. Later infills of boulder clay have helped form the valley as it is today.

3. Cwm yr Eglwys (the valley of the church), like it's close neighbour Pwllgwaelod, is one of the most popular beaches on the northern coast, but unlike Pwllgwaelod with it's grey sand, has fine golden sand at low water. The 15th century church, of which only the western wall and belfry survive, was destroyed, along with low lying cottages and the quay, in a truly ferocious storm in October 1859 which wrecked shipping all around the Welsh coast. Of the 114 ships wrecked the worst was the *Royal Charter*, sunk off Anglesey with the loss of 459 lives. A new church was built on safer grounds, inland at Brynhenllan, in 1860. Like it's predecessor it was dedicated to the 6th century St Brynach. One of the many coastal trading ports Cwm yr Eglwys was, at least in the late 18th century, known as Dinas Harbour. Sheltered as it is from the prevailing westerlies, the cove shows a marked difference in appearance to Pwllgwaelod. Trees and shrubs flourish here, adding their softer greens to the blues and greys of the sea and sky.

4. The attraction here is Needle Rock, the great sea stack which provides a grand home for breeding guillemots and razorbills from April to July. With the clamour of breeding kittiwakes and gulls, jackdaws and fulmars this can be a noisy and entertaining place. Watch for the great black-backed gulls attempting to knock eggs off the ledges for food! There are usually a few young fulmars, hatched on the cliffs below, present until September, but most sea birds have by then left to overwinter at sea. Great views from here of Newport Bay, with Cardigan Island and the great rock folds of Cemaes Head and Pen yr Afr in sight on clear days, with inland Carn Ingli and Newport village, the castle and church tower just visible.

5. Dinas Head, or rather Pen y Fan (the top of the peak), stands at 466 feet/142 metres high. It's survival as a headland is due to the Silurian grits of which it is partly formed, harder rock than the surrounding softer Ordovician shales and sandstones which have fallen victim to the sea's adventuring. There are the ruins of a former Coastguard lookout by the OS trig point. In addition to Newport Bay there are magnificent views west over Fishguard Bay

to Garn Fawr and Strumble Head, and inland to Dinas and the outlying hills of the Preseli range. Fishguard Bay's history as a harbour began with the opening of the new harbour in 1908. Fishguard offers the shortest crossing to Ireland from anywhere in Wales or England, and a new steamer service to Rosslare was inaugurated. For a short time, before 1914, Cunard used Fishguard as the terminus for their New York sailings, nudging for berthing space with the liners of the Booth and Blue Funnel lines. However transatlantic sailings were not resumed after 1918, and nowadays a car ferry to Rosslare is it's busiest traffic. From the headland there are good chances of seeing seals in the waters below, perhaps even a harbour porpoise or dolphin. Local tales tell of a fisherman who when he cast anchor off the headland received an unexpected visitor. One of the fairy folk, the Bendith y Mamau, who had their city under the sea here, climbed up the anchor rope and complained the anchor had gone through his roof! Dinas Island Farm, some 400 acres, was once the Elizabethan grange which provided game for the formerly splendid Pentre Ifan mansion, near Newport. Recent holders have included the naturalist Ronald Lockley, raising cattle, sheep, corn and early potatoes.

Walk Directions: [-] denotes Point of Interest

1. Starting from Pwllgwaelod [1] follow the valley path along Cwm Dewi [2] the 0.5 miles/0.75 kilometres to Cwm yr Eglwys. The path, suitable for wheelchairs, leads off from just behind the row of buildings by the car park.

2. Once at Cwm yr Eglwys [3] follow the tarmac road as it goes left uphill. Almost immediately turn right over a footbridge onto the Coast Path.

3. Follow the Coast Path uphill, passing Needle Rock [4], to reach Dinas Head [5]. From here it is an easy descent to Pwllgwaelod and the starting point.

Facilities:

Parking also possible at Cwm yr Eglwys, where there is a small charge.

Pwllgwaelod has public toilets, as does Cwm yr Eglwys. There is a licensed restaurant at Pwllgwaelod, open during the holiday season, which does bar meals during the day. Other facilities are available in Dinas.

Pwll Deri - Strumble Head - Carreg Wastad Point - Tre Howel - Garngilfach - Garn Fawr - Pwll Deri

May be treated as 2 separate walks if preferred, using the road to Strumble Head as a link path: Pwll Deri - Strumble Head - Garn Fawr - Pwll Deri 5.5 miles/9 kilometres, Strumble Head - Carreg Wastad Point - Tre Howel - Strumble Head 6 miles/9.5 kilometres.

OS Maps:	1:50 000 St David's and Haverfordwest 157; 1:25 000 Outdoor Leisure 35 North Pembrokeshire/Fishguard (Abergwaun) 1032 (SM 83/93).
Start:	Pwll Deri. Strumble Head would make an alternative starting point, plenty of parking space available as at Pwll Deri.
Access:	Pwll Deri is 5.5 miles/9 kilometres from Fishguard. Can also be reached from the south through St Nicholas. No buses.
Parking:	Parking bay at Pwll Deri.
Grade:	Strenuous — mainly coastal path, farm track and green lane.

Points of Interest:

1. Pwll Deri, pool of the oak trees, is as attractive as the name suggests, with the sheer cliffs dropping down to the seal bright sea, and the rock headland striding down to St David's Head. Not many oak trees though, too windy for that! A popular place for those who like their scenery wild and dramatic. There is a memorial here to the Welsh poet Dewi Emrys, who immortalised Pwll Deri in a poem written in the local dialect. The landscape to

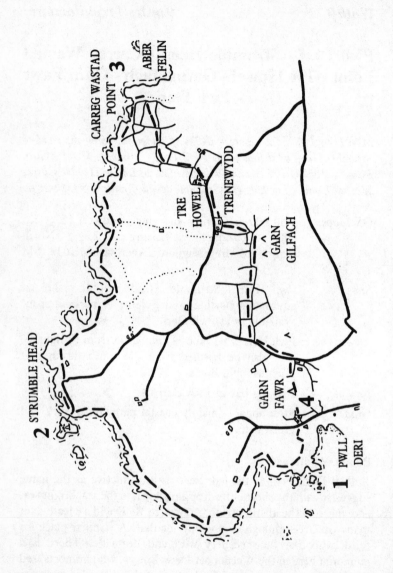

2 STRUMBLE HEAD

CARREG WASTAD POINT 3

ABER FELIN

TRE HOWEL

TRENEWYDD

GARN GILFACH

GARN FAWR

4

1 PWLL DERI

Strumble Head and beyond is one of igneous headlands, intercut with bays where the softer sedimentary rocks predominate. Dinas Mawr, as might be expected from it's strategic position, was once an Iron Age fort, protected on it's landward side by double banks. Trefasser is believed to be the birthplace of Bishop Asser, the 9th century friend, counsellor and chronicler of the Anglo-Saxon king of Wessex, Alfred the Great — he who burnt the cakes! Asser spent his youth studying at St David's monastic community, from where he was enlisted for service by Alfred, dividing his time from circa 885 onwards between the court and St David's. En route to Strumble Head, just before the derelict Ministry of Defence buildings, steps have been cut down to the beach of Porth Maenmelyn through a cleft dynamited out by a Mr Clark, one of the engineers who worked on Fishguard Harbour in 1908, and who lived in the house which is now the youth hostel. Just the kind of hidden and lonely place to be made use of by smugglers! Access to the beach is guarded by a metal gate.

2. Strumble Head is dominated by it's splendid lighthouse. Built by Trinity House in 1908 at the time Fishguard Harbour was being built, it's location on Ynys Meicel was seen as ideal for guiding ships safely around to the new harbour. Nowadays the lighthouse is automatic, monitored from St Ann's Head light. Access is across a narrow footbridge, but no visitors allowed! Light visibility is good for over 31 nautical miles, it's booming foghorn audible for 5 nautical miles. Strumble Head is a noted location for bird and sea watchers, with spring and autumn bird migrations, and the early morning and late evening summer passage of Manx shearwaters skimming low over the water from their breeding sites on the Pembrokeshire islands to feeding sites in Cardigan Bay. An old Ministry of Defence building has been converted to provide basic shelter for sea watchers. There is a Coastguard station, still manned, nearby.

Allez France!

Following the great Revolution in France in 1789, the consequent Reign of Terror and the fall of Robespierre in

1794, power in France was administered from 1795 to 1799 by the Directory. Continuing the war begun in April 1792 against Austria the Directory devised a plan to deal with her 2 main enemies of the time: England and Austria. An English backed landing of French emigrés at Brittany in 1795 had been easily defeated by the Army of the West under General Lazare Hoche, one result of the victory being the acquisition of thousands of British uniforms and rifles which were to be used against England. It was proposed to conduct a war of privateers against the English, with landings on Irish and British soil to ferment anarchy and provide support for rebels.

In December 1796 Hoche's army of 15,000 left Brest for Bantry Bay in Ireland, but was unable to land, like the Spanish Armada of 200 years or so before, because of storms. On 16 February 1797 a further expedition of 1400 men, the Légion Noire under the command of an Irish-American with experience of fighting in the American War of Independence, a Colonel Tate, left Brittany, bound for either Bristol or South Wales. Unable to land at Bristol the expedition of 4 ships sailed on, rounding St David's Head on Wednesday, 22 February 1797. Recognised, and forced out of Fishguard Bay by a single shot from Fishguard Fort, it was decided to take advantage of the calm weather and moonlit night, and accordingly the men (in the now dyed British uniforms) and stores were landed at the steep cliffs of Carreg Wastad Point.

As planned the ships returned to France, while Colonel Tate set up his headquarters at Tre Howel Farm. Transport and food now being the requirement the men — mainly grenadiers and ex-convicts — set out to scour Pencaer peninsula. January 1797 had seen a Portuguese coaster wrecked off the coast, and the majority of farms in the area had fine Portuguese wine in addition to cattle, pigs, poultry and sheep. Here the invasion started to go wrong, and the motley assortment of troops, making no attempt at concealment, decided to liberate the wine instead of the local populace! As a result several hundred of the invasion force deserted camp en masse.

By this time panic was spreading throughout the area, with both locals and French killed and injured. Fortunately the heroes of the hour were close at hand in the shape of Lord Cawdor of Stackpole and his Castlemartin Yeomanry, who, on hearing of the invasion, had marched north, collecting all able bodied men en route. They arrived at Fishguard early in the evening of the 23rd, ready to face the French, who were now deployed on the cliffs overlooking Goodwick. The night being particularly dark, the drums were sounded for recall, and Lord Cawdor's men retreated. The French, thinking the drums sounded the advance, also retreated, firing as they went! Stalemate.

Lord Cawdor's men in their blue uniforms had already been sighted by the French before they reached Fishguard, yet it is said the French also saw, silhouetted against the gun dark sky, another force dressed in red. These are believed to have been the local women who had gathered on the hills in their red cloaks, to act as spectators or soldiers as necessary. Cometh the hour, cometh the heroine, and one Jemima Nicholas of Fishguard, not content to be a spectator, marched into battle with a pitchfork, rounded up 12 Frenchmen, and marched them off to Fishguard guardhouse.

The combination of events, desertions and dissatisfied officers had led Tate, by late on the Thursday evening, to sue for peace. Terms were agreed and the surrender signed on the morning of Friday, 24 February 1797 at the Royal Oak in Fishguard — the table on which they signed is still there, with other memorabilia of events. The force accordingly marched down to Goodwick sands in the afternoon, and were escorted south to imprisonment in Haverfordwest's castle and churches. Among the French was James Bowen, formerly a servant at Tre Howel Farm who had been transported for horse stealing, and who had joined the force at Brest. No doubt his presence had influenced the choice of Carreg Wastad Point, and the use of Tre Howel Farm as the French headquarters.

All in all the Directory's campaign against England had proved to be a failure, as it had against Austria, that is with one notable exception. On the Italian Campaign General Napoleon Bonaparte swept all before him, a feat he was to repeat in 1799 when he swept the Directory away into European history, opening a new chapter in French — English relations!

* * *

3. Carreg Wastad is famous as the site of the last invasion of Britain in February 1797. The memorial stone was erected in 1897, in commemoration of the glorious event. There is a 100 foot/30.4 metres long tapestry depicting events, and created as a community project for the 2nd anniversary in 1997 — on display in Fishguard. The sheltered shingle beaches of Aber Felin bay are ideal for the local grey seals. Pupping takes place from September to December, with each female dropping a single pup, and the inaccessibility of the bay provides a safe and protected site. Goods views north east of the sloping flat top of Dinas Island, and on to Cemaes Head and Cardigan Island.

4. At 699 feet/213 metres Garn Fawr is the highest point on Pencaer peninsula. An early Iron Age fort is it's crowning glory, with at least 3 ramparts still traceable. Entrance would have been from the eastern, more accessible side. However the stones have been borrowed and moved around so much that the original layout is difficult to determine. There was a radar station here during World War 2, but now only the walls remain. Glorious views of the table top peninsula below, neatly divided up into pocket handkerchief sized fields, with attendant white wall dwellings and farms. Inland the great Lion Rock of Treffgarne gorge turns away from the Preselis towards St Brides Bay and the islands. In Tal y Gaer

farmyard is an early stone beehive hut, described variously as an early monk's cell, and, unkindly, as a prehistoric pigsty. It is to the left of the stile as you enter the farmyard from the heights of Garn Fawr, partly covered in bracken and grass. Just room enough to stand up in!

Walk Directions: [-] denotes Point of Interest

1. From Pwll Deri [1] join the Coast Path and continue the 3 miles/5 kilometres or so to Strumble Head [2].

2. From Strumble Head continue on the Coast Path to Carreg Wastad Point [3]. This section is also just under 3 miles/5 kilometres; the neat whitewashed cottage of Penrhyn marking the halfway point.

3. From Carreg Wastad Point follow the Coast Path to reach a stile. Cross the stile, but do not turn left. Instead leave the Coast Path and go straight up the carn in front on an undefined path.

4. Stay in this rough field — mainly gorse — and go ahead to the top left of the field to reach 2 stone gatepost pillars. Go through into another field, and keeping to the left field edge, continue to reach a farm lane.

5. Go ahead on the farm lane, ignoring the first lane right, to reach a T junction with another farm lane. Bear right, and continue through Tre Howel Farm to reach the minor road to Strumble Head. Tre Howel Farm acted as the French headquarters during the brief invasion of 1797.

6. Bear right and continue to Trenewydd. Turn left here, and go between the farmhouse and the barn to join a farm lane leading uphill.

7. Continue uphill to reach a T junction with another lane/path. Turn right, and continue, keeping the dry stone wall/hedge to your right. Garngilfach will now be above left.

8. Continue to reach a farm gate giving access to a green lane. Go ahead on the green lane to reach a minor road.

9. Turn left and continue uphill on the minor road to reach a small

car park on the right. Turn right onto the footpath by the car park — signposted 'Public Footpath' — and continue uphill to Garn Fawr [4].

10. From Garn Fawr descend straight down through Tal y Gaer Farm to Pwll Deri and the starting point.

Facilties:

Parking also possible at Strumble Head, and at the small car park on the landward side of Garn Fawr.

Youth hostel and campaign site at Pwll Deri, BT telephone at Trefasser. No other facilities.

Abercastle - Carnachen Lwyd - Morfa - Pen yr Allt Wood - Aber Mawr - Pwllstrodur - Abercastle

OS Maps:	1:50 000 St David's and Haverfordwest 157; 1:25 000 Outdoor Leisure 35 North Pembrokeshire/ Fishguard (Abergwaun) 1032 (SM 83/93).
Start:	Abercastle.
Access:	Abercastle is situated on the coast, 2 miles/3 kilometres north west of Mathry, and 1 mile/1.5 kilometres north east of Trefin. Nearest bus service 411 stops at Trefin and Mathry en route from St David's to Fishguard.
Parking:	There is a small parking area by the foreshore in Abercastle.
Grade:	Moderate — green lane, woodland and coastal path, some road walking.

Points of Interest:

1. Sheltered behind the delightfully named Cwm Badau — valley of the boats, is the cove of Abercastle, a pretty village of colour washed cottages. Hard to believe now, but this was once a bustling little sea port, with ships from Liverpool and Bristol unloading anthracite and general merchandise, leaving with corn and butter. There were 3 vessels ranging from 25 to 34 tons built here between 1790 and 1820, and certainly local sloops based in the cove in the early 19th century were involved in national trade — perhaps a little smuggling also! The farmlands around Mathry are noted as some of the richest in the county, and no doubt imported anthracite was used to fire the limekiln at the head of the beach to provide the lime needed to sweeten the soil. There are 2 bollards

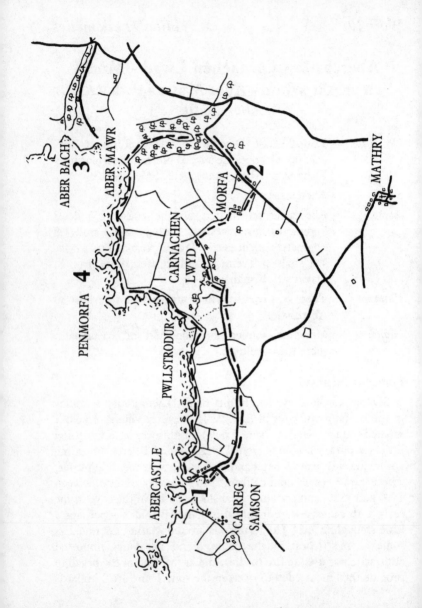

ABERCASTLE

PWLLSTRODUR

PENMORFA **4**

ABER MAWR

ABER BACH **3**

CARNACHEN LWYD

MORFA

2

MATHRY

1

CARREG SAMSON

nearby which once saw service as canons! The ruined building on the headland to the right is the old granary. Coastal trade continued until the 1920s, when road transport came into the ascendancy.

Neolithic man was here some 5000 years ago, leaving behind him the superb cromlech, or burial chamber, of Carreg Samson, certainly one of the best examples in the county. Only 3 of it's pillars are left, supporting the capstone of 16ft/5m by 9ft/3m. Originally the whole structure would have been covered by earth and pebbles, and may well have been used for over a 100 separate burials. Local tradition has it that the cromlech was in fact built by Samson, who, show-off that he was, raised the capstone into place with his little finger. Unfortunately this gladiatorial feat did not quite work, for Samson lost his finger in the process. In memorium the finger was buried on Ynys Castell, the island guarding Abercastle's right flank, and the island is accordingly known as the grave of Samson's finger. The cromlech can easily be reached on the footpath leading inland from the Coast Path by Cwm Badau. Situated on Longhouse Farm the farm itself was once a grange of the Bishop of St David's, who had a Palace, now untraceable, at nearby Trefin. Abercastle is nowadays a sailing and shellfishing harbour, many of it's homes holiday cottages. Sadly of it's 3 former pubs none now remain!

First Across the Atlantic

On 10 August, 1876 residents of Abercastle were surprised by the arrival of a 24 year old American. It was not that visitors were uncommon, trading ships frequently called from Liverpool and Bristol, what was different was that the American had arrived in an 18 foot boat, was clearly in want of food, and had sailed not from a British port or cove but had sailed single-handed across the Atlantic from Massachusetts, USA.

The American was Alfred Johnson, a fisherman from Gloucester, Massachusetts. It was the centenary of the birth of the United States, and he had decided to celebrate. To prove the greatness of the American seaman he decided to sail alone across the Atlantic to visit his relations in Liverpool. He named his boat '*Centennial*', and set sail from Gloucester on 15 June, 1876. After a brief stop in Nova Scotia and a capsizing in August he duly arrived, by chance, in Abercastle. After 2 days rest he continued on his sea journey, joining his family in Liverpool on 17 August, 1876.

The first man to sail single-handed across the Atlantic returned home by less hazardous means. His arrival went unheralded and unnoticed, and he quietly resumed his life as a fisherman on the Grand Banks.

★ ★ ★

2. From here good views inland of Mathry, a fine example of a medieval hilltop village, though there would certainly have been earlier settlements. It's dominant position in the area made it an ideal choice for trade and commerce, and markets and fairs were held here for centuries; the right to hold markets regularised by charter under Edward III in the 14th century. The origin of the name Mathry may be a corruption of martyr — in Welsh the name would be 'Merthyr'. The story is that on one day a Pembrokeshire woman gave birth to 7 children — a source of joy and wonder to the mother perhaps, but one of sorrow to the father, who, unable to support them, vowed to drown them in the river Taf. However they were saved in the nick of time by St Teilo, each of them being henceforth provided for by the daily appearance of a large fish by the water's edge. Eventually the 7 children came to live in Mathry. The church is accordingly dedicated to the 7 saints.

3. The approach to Aber Mawr is through Pen yr Allt wood, a pleasant wood of oak, ash, and hazel. During the Mesolithic period this wooded landscape would have stretched far out to sea, but as sea levels rose the land disappeared beneath the waters. The fossilised remnants of this forest can be seen at low tides. The storm beach of shingle and stone is more recent, having been thrown up during a ferocious storm in 1859 which destroyed well

over 100 ships in it's wild passage across land and sea. That well known Victorian in his stove pipe hat was here in the 1840s — Isambard Kingdom Brunel was hatching another engineering feat on behalf of the Great Western Railway (GWR). It was planned to run the South Wales Railway, formed in 1844 as small brother and project of the GWR, from Cardiff to Swansea, Carmarthen and Fishguard, to connect with steamboats for Ireland. Then, in 1846, came the terrible Irish potato famine and the proposed route to Fishguard was scrapped — little business opportunity was foreseen in the shattered country.

Then, for some reason, whether it was Aber Mawr's softer rock, or the fact that payment from the GWR was to be paid only on completion of the railway, Brunel shifted his proposed terminus to Aber Mawr. Abutments for piers were built at Penmorfa and Carreg Golchfa, and an incline for rail track laid down — the traces are still there for the keen-eyed. However, in 1851, as soon as he had arrived, Brunel was gone, work abandoned, and Neyland chosen as the new terminal. Connection was made with Ireland eventually — a submarine telegraph cable was laid across the Irish Sea in 1883 from what is now a private dwelling by Aber Bach's parking bay. Fishguard had to wait until 1908 before she got her Irish ferry connection. Aber Mawr and Aber Bach are now popular and uncrowded beaches, both good for swimming and exploration.

4. Penmorfa has a fine Iron Age fort, Castell Coch, dating from circa 300 B.C. The fort was protected by 2 ditches and 3 walls, with a zig zag entrance. The outer wall is an 18th century field wall, the stone wall exposed underneath the overlying turf. Great views north to Strumble Head. It was from here that Brunel planned to send out one of his piers into Aber Mawr bay.

Walk Directions: [-] denotes Point of Interest

1. Starting from Abercastle [1] walk uphill on the minor road towards Mathry.

2. After passing Brynawelon on your left turn left onto the minor

road leading to Carnachen-lwyd — there is a 'No Through Road' sign here.

3. Continue to Carnachen-lwyd — great views open up of Strumble Head and the coast. Just before Carnachen-lwyd is reached there is a public footpath on the left giving access to the tiny cove of Pwllstrodur.

4. Once at Carnachen-lwyd turn left onto the green lane — there is a sign here of a horse and rider, indicating the route is a bridleway.

5. Continue on the green lane/bridleway to join a farm track. This route was once the old county road to Aber Mawr until part of it was washed away.

6. After a short distance turn right onto the farm track leading to Morfa Farm.

7. At the farm buildings turn right and then left, and continue on the farm road to join the minor road to Aber Mawr and St Nicholas [2]. The public footpath indicated on the OS maps (other than Outdoor Leisure), which passes to the left of the Morfa Farm buildings, is now too overgrown to be walked.

8. Turn left and follow the minor road downhill. Go through the farmgate just before the road bends sharp right — the gate is marked with the National Trust sign, and 'Aber Mawr'.

9. There is the choice now of following the bridleway, or the public footpath across a field, and then up a ladder stile to join a woodland path. The bridleway can be wet underfoot in winter.

10. Continue on either route to Aber Mawr's storm beach [3].

11. At Aber Mawr turn left and join the Coast Path. Follow the Path to Penmorfa [4] and Pwllstrodur, and on to Abercastle and the starting point. There is a boundary wall skirting the coast as you approach Abercastle — someone has neatly inscribed in the mortar 'The Great Wall of China'. Remember, you saw it here first!

Facilities:

Limited parking possible at Aber Bach, Aber Mawr's sister bay.

BT telephone kiosk, post box, seasonal public toilets at Abercastle. No other facilities, nearest at Trefin on the coast 1 mile/1.5 kilometres away which offers a pub, shop, youth hostel and B & B accommodation, or inland at Mathry 2 miles/3 kilometres away, offering a Post Office and general store, pub, and B & B accommodation. Less than a mile inland from Aber Mawr is Tregwynt woollen mill, still producing the traditional Welsh weaves — worth a visit.

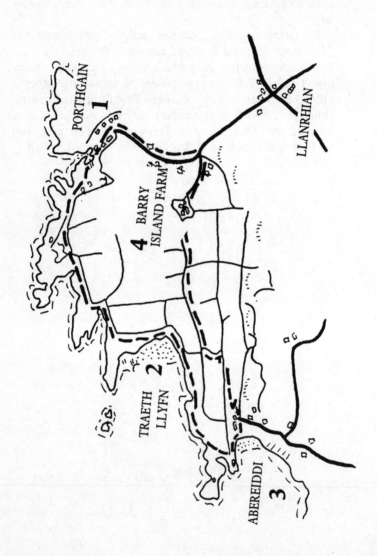

Porthgain - Traeth Llyfn - Abereiddi - Barry Island Farm - Porthgain

OS Maps:	1:50 000 St David's and Haverfordwest 157; 1:25 000 Outdoor Leisure 35 North Pembrokeshire/Fishguard (Agergwaun) 1032 (SM 83/93), St David's (Tyddewi) and Ramsey Island 1055 (SM 62/72).
Start:	Coast Path at Porthgain.
Access:	Porthgain is situated on the coast halfway between St David's and Strumble Head. From Croesgoch, situated on the A487 St David's to Goodwick road, take the minor road leading to Llanrhian and Porthgain. Bus 411 stops at Llanrhian, en route from St David's to Fishguard.
Parking:	There is a car park in Porthgain, in front of the Sloop Inn.
Grade:	Easy — coastal path, field, farm track and road.

Points of Interest:

1. Anyone visiting Porthgain for the first time will immediately be aware of the imposing ruins marching up the cliff face from the harbour. A visitor 160 years or so ago would have seen none of this, perhaps only a huddle of fishing boats drawn up on a different shoreline, for Porthgain's harbour owes it's present shape to man-made construction. Porthgain's geology has given the area an identity and industrial history unique in Pembrokeshire. The metamorphosed shale here gave slate for flooring and roofing, the clay was used for brick making, and the volcanic dolerite rock provided roadstone for Britain's developing roads. Porthgain's industrial revolution started in 1837 when George Le Hunte, the local landowner, granted a lease to a local company to extract flags,

slates and stones. However it was a London consortium, Barclay & Company, who were granted other leases in 1840, who started the transformation. The first harbour was built, the first quarries were developed, and the first tramway joining nearby Abereiddi and it's slate quarry to Porthgain harbour was laid. Brick making had to wait until 1878, when, under the St Brides Slate & Slab Co., Porthgain's heavier than normal bricks began to find their way to places as far afield as Dublin and Bridgwater. By 1912, after several changes of ownership, there were 3 steam locomotives, plus traction engines and motor lorry, on site. One loco, the 'Charger', had seen service in the Jarrow shipyards, the others were the 'Singapore', and appropriately, as first engine, the 'Porthgain'.

The slate and brick industries here fell into decline by the early 1900s, and crushed stone took on greater importance. Small pieces of blasted stone were hauled up the 'Jerusalem Road' from Porthgain's quarry and crushed into sizes from 0.25 to 2.5 inches and stored in the hoppers. They were then exported by company ship or road. By 1931 fortunes declined, and in August of that year business closed. There are still extensive ruins worth exploration. The present restaurant was the former company offices, and Tŷ Mawr, the recently restored building adjacent to the green, was connected with brick making. The stone chutes and hoppers dominate the harbour, and the old tunnel cut through to Porthgain's slate quarry can be easily picked out. On the cliffs above are the ruins of the former quarrymen's cottages, and the loco shed, weighbridge and water tower still partially stand. The extensive quarry and ruined smithy can be explored from the 'Jerusalem Road'. The village is now in local ownership, with the harbour, quarries and cliff land the responsibility of the National Park.

2. Traeth Llyfn, translated as the smooth, or sleek beach, has a fine sandy beach. Good for swimming, though there is a strong outgoing current, noticeably to the left. From the headlands around Traeth Llyfn the rock outcrops of Carn Llidi and Pen Beri appear as truly imposing mountains dominating St David's Head.

St Finbar is said to have sailed from here to found the city of Cork, while Columba sailed en route to Iona.

3. The slate quarry here at Abereiddi was part and parcel of Porthgain's industrial enterprise. The poor harbour, vessels of only 20 to 30 tons could load from the quarry slip, meant that the construction of a tramway to Porthgain harbour was essential. In length just under 2 miles, trains, consisting of usually 2 or 3 wagons, were hauled by 2 horses to the Slate Yard near Barry Island Farm for storage, before being shipped out. The quarry was at it's busiest from circa 1850 to 1904, with exports of Abereiddi and Porthgain slate to Bristol Channel and English Channel ports. The ruins of the engine house, the dressing sheds, and the quarrymen's cottages known as 'The Row', are still evident. Sometime after quarrying had ceased the connecting walls leading from the old engine house around to the dressing sheds were blasted away, resulting in a small harbour, well known locally as 'The Blue Lagoon' — the water truly is blue! The bay is famous in geological circles for the fossil graptolites found in it's Ordovician slates when split. A first was recorded here with the discovery of a previously unknown example of these plant-like animals. There is a possibly 18th century observation tower on Trwyn Castell Head overlooking Abereiddi Bay. A curious building, there is even a fireplace inside should you need to get warm! Like many remote headlands on the Pembrokeshire coast Trwyn Castell would have been home to Iron Age settlers.

4. Barry Island takes it's name from a geological feature of the landscape, hinted at by the narrow valley along which the tramway from Abereiddi ran. As the Ice Age came to an end the Irish Sea ice melted, and a sub glacial meltwater channel was formed which ran down to Abereiddi Bay and provided temporary island status. Dinas Island, near Newport, owes it's landscape charter to similar action.

Walk Directions: [-] denotes Point of Interest

1. From the car park in Porthgain [1] walk down to the harbour and

bear left, passing in front of the old stone chutes. By the stone building (the former Pilot House) climb the steps to reach the gate giving access to the headland.

2. Go through the gate, passing the National Trust stone box on your left. To the right, on the headland, there is a stone pillar, matched by another on the opposite side of the harbour — these mark the harbour entrance, and are currently painted white.

3. Continue on the path. After a short distance the path breaks in two. Keep to the left hand path — the right, known as the Jerusalem Road, leads downhill to the old quarry and the ruins of the smithy.

4. Keep to the level path, passing to the left above the quarry, and follow the Coast Path as it continues left around to the wooden footbridge and stile giving access to Traeth Llyfn [2]. Stone and metal steps lead down to the beach. There is car parking available here in season, access through Barry Island Farm. It is a popular beach!

5. Continue on the Coast Path as it bears right around the beach headland, and follow it on to Abereiddi [3].

6. Once at Abereiddi head inland from the beach, keeping the ruined quarrymen's cottages on your immediate left, to reach the wooden stile by the public toilets.

7. Almost immediately after crossing the stile you will need to take the short path leading back, left and uphill to reach the old tramway cutting once used for transporting slate.

8. Turn right and follow the farm track (the original tramway route, now lost, led downhill to the valley) uphill to reach a wooden stile.

9. Cross the wooden stile into a field, and keeping to the right field edge continue to a field gate. Ignore the stile in front of you — this leads back to the coast — and instead continue right on a farm track.

10. Follow the farm track through Barry Island Farm [4] to reach the minor road leading to Porthgain.

11. At the minor road turn left, and continue downhill to Porthgain and the starting point.

Facilities:

Parking is also possible at Abereiddi, and seasonal parking available at Traeth Llyfn (access through Barry Island Farm).

There is a pub and a restaurant in Porthgain, as well as public toilets and a BT telephone. Public toilets, emergency telephone, and seasonal ice cream van in Abereiddi! Barry Island now offer a 'Country Hotel and Holiday Centre', with refreshments and accommodation available.

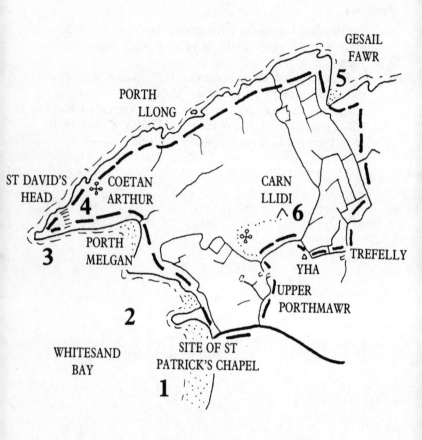

GESAIL
FAWR

PORTH
LLONG

5

ST DAVID'S
HEAD

COETAN
ARTHUR

CARN
LLIDI

4

^ **6**

3

PORTH
MELGAN

TREFELLY

YHA

UPPER
PORTHMAWR

2

WHITESAND
BAY

SITE OF ST
PATRICK'S CHAPEL

1

Whitesand Bay - Porth Melgan - St David's Head - Coetan Arthur - Gesail Fawr - Trefelly - Upper Porthmawr - Whitesand Bay

OS Maps:	1:50 000 St David's and Haverfordwest 157; 1:25 000 Outdoor Leisure 35 North Pembrokeshire/St David's (Tyddewi) and Ramsey Island 1055 (SM 62/72).
Start:	Coast Path at Whitesand Bay car park.
Access:	Whitesand Bay is reached on the B4583 from St David's. Nearest public transport access point at St David's.
Parking:	Whitesand Bay car park — seasonal charge.
Grade:	Moderate — coastal path, field and track.

Points of Interest:

1. Whitesand Bay. The Welsh name Traeth Mawr means *great beach*. It's golden sands make it a popular place in summer. Popular also with surfers and canoeists all year round — the bay is one of the best surfing beaches in Wales. Boats leave from here for trips around Ramsey Island in the high season. At exceptionally low tides there are the remains of a prehistoric forest, as well as those of the wreck of the paddle tug *Guiding Star*, aground in 1882. Porth Melgan, by St David's Head, provides a less hectic, but equally rewarding summer beach. Popular fiction has gifted Cornwall with it's fair share of coastal smuggling. However Cornwall was not alone. An 1807 account notes the arrest of a smuggling vessel in Whitesand Bay by the Coastguard cutter *Hope*. The crew had been in the process of transferring a cargo of spirits into smaller casks. The empty casks would have been brought out from local shores, quite possibly from the comparative safety of

Ramsey Island. Surely an indication of a booming local trade!

2. During the 5th and 6th centuries Wales experienced the full force of the monastic movement — truly the Age of the Saints. St David, a Pembrokeshire man and Wales' patron saint, established his church and monastery in the nearby city in around 550. One aspect of this monastic movement was the continual travelling of both saints and disciples on missionary journeys between not only the emergent Celtic nations, but also to places as far afield as Iceland. It was customary to pray for delivery from danger prior to sea journeys, and similarly to give thanks after the journey, using wherever possible wide sandy beaches for the landing. Chapels, dedicated to the saints, began to dot the Celtic coastline. St Patrick, Ireland's patron saint, reputedly sailed from Whitesand Bay to Ireland, and the chapel built on the site was dedicated to him. Nothing now remains but the site, however the area was excavated in the 1920s and the skeleton of a young man found. There is a plaque at the site which, just decipherable, reads 'Underneath lies a chapel dedicated to St Patrick. Built 6th-10th century. Excavated 1924'.

St David's Settlement and Cathedral

St David founded his church and monastery in the mid 6th century, though nothing remains of the foundations. Property was held in common, with emphasis on prayer and simple sustenance through water and a primarily vegetarian diet. Pilgrims, arriving by road and sea, flocked to St David's throughout the Middle Ages. On the pilgrimage route from Ireland to Santiago de Compostela in Spain via Wales, Cornwall and Brittany, it was said that 2 pilgrimages to St David's was equal to one to Rome, 3 the equal of one to Jerusalem. The settlement survived the frequent Viking raids, but it's importance was seen as a threat by the incoming Normans, who imposed their own pattern of cathedral and diocese.

William the Conqueror paid homage here in 1081. David himself was canonized in 1120. The present cathedral,

Wales' finest church, was begun circa 1182, reaching completion 340 years later in 1522. The core of the building is late 12th century, but many later alterations have given the exterior 14th century styling. There is a fine Irish oak ceiling in the nave, dating from 1500. The miseres in the choir stalls date from the mid 15th century. There have been various restorations since completion. The addition of the local Caerfai sandstone has given the exterior a purplish overtone. The ruined Bishop's Palace nearby was largely built between 1280 and 1350 by Bishop Gower. Abetted by the Reformation the palace was derelict by the 18th century.

* * *

3. There is a fine Iron Age promontory fort on St David's Head, protected by the remnants of the Clawdd y Milwyr — the Warrior's Dyke. The original inner rampart would have been 15ft/4.5m high by 12ft/3.5m thick at the base, with 2 smaller walls and 3 ditches. The entrance would have been across a causeway and through a 7ft/2m wide passageway. Dated to 100 AD the site may have developed over 2 different periods. Within the settlement, at the foot of a rock outcrop, clearly visible are 8 hut circles, the remains of circular stone houses which would have been thatched with bracken, rushes or grass. These provided the living quarters. There are the remains of a stone wall stretching obliquely across the headland from Porth Llong a quarter of a mile/half a kilometre away, defining a wider settlement area. Probably making their living by mixed farming and stock breeding the Iron Age settlers may have used this area for stock as well as for living. The Porth Melgan valley and the western slopes of Carn Llidi may have been used as fields. Evidence of stone field boundaries are there on the valley slopes, but are probably of a later date. Worthy of exploration the area is now haunted only by the cries of gulls, oystercatchers, and the local choughs.

4. Prior to the arrival of Iron Age settlers the area was occupied by Neolithic immigrants. Arriving from 3,000 BC onwards they lived by crop raising and animal herding. Little remains of their flimsy

houses, what have survived are the cromlechau, the stone burial chambers. Originally covered by earth or stones, with the upright pillars infilled with dry stone walling, only their stone structures survive. Coetan Arthur — Arthur's quoit — has been dated to circa 3,000 BC. There are the remains of 2 other burial chambers on the western slope of Carn Llidi, one with it's capstone dislodged. Later peoples, not knowing the history of prehistoric monuments, came to associate them with the heroes of legend; Arthur, Samson and the Devil strode the landscape, and the Druids made human sacrifice on the capstones.

5. The near inaccessibility of Gesail Fawr is typical of the indented northern Pembrokeshire coastline and the Pembrokeshire islands. However this inaccessibility is good news for the grey seals. These remote beaches, including Gesail Fawr, are the scene of frenetic activity when in autumn the females come ashore to drop a single pup. The male will protect a harem of 5 to 10 females. Diving seals normally stay under water for 5 minutes or so, however a dive can last for up to 20 minutes. So if you are waiting for a seal to re-surface you may have a long wait!

6. It is well worth taking time out for the ascent of Carn Llidi — easily climbed from it's western side. The views from the summit can be breathtaking. From the summit the flatness of the landscape becomes obvious. The plateau would have been formed as a result of constant wave action at a time when the land was beneath the sea. Only the harder igneous outcrops such as Carn Llidi would have resisted the wave erosion. The track leading to the lesser summit was built during World War 1 and led to a hydrophone station which detected enemy submarines. In World War 2 the site was extended to become a radar station with scanners on Carn Llidi. Only the base of the buildings now remain. The 2 cromlechau noted at Point 4 are to the right of the track, just below the lesser summit.

Walk Directions: [-] denotes Point of Interest

1. From Whitesand Bay [1] car park join the Coast Path at the

wooden gate to the right of the 2 BT telephone kiosks. The route is clearly signposted 'Coast Path'.

2. Follow the Coast Path uphill, passing the site of St Patrick's chapel on your left [2], and continue on to Porth Melgan and St David's Head [3] 1 mile/1.5 kilometres away.

3. From St David's Head fork left, passing Coetan Arthur on your right [4], and continue for a mile/1.5 kilometres to reach a stile set into a stone wall.

4. Cross the stile and continue on the Coast Path, passing above Gesail Fawr [5] to another stile. Cross the stile and shortly leave the Coast Path, bearing right and uphill. There is a footpath sign here, indicating 'Public Footpath'. There is to the left, overlooking the sea, the deserted Quaker village of Maes y Mynydd.

5. Continue uphill on the path to meet another path at the top of the rise. Bear right to shortly join a green lane bearing left.

6. At the end of the green lane bear right to a field gate and stile — great views of Ramsey Island and Skomer Island framing St Brides Bay!

7. Cross the stile and bear diagonally left to meet the farm lane leading to Trefelly.

8. Continue down the lane until just before the farm access gate. Cross right a stile leading into a field.

9. Cross 2 fields to reach the youth hostel. Turn right here and continue up a lane to a stile giving access on to the footpath skirting Carn Llidi [6] — a most imposing view!

10. Turn left and continue to meet the farm lane leading down to Upper Porthmawr. Turn left and follow the track through the farm and down to the road leading to Whitesand Bay.

11. Bear right and return to the car park and starting point.

Facilities:

Whitesand Bay has a seasonal shop and café, public toilets, emergency and BT telephones, as well as a seasonal lifeguard hut and First Aid point. There is also a camping and caravan site, and a youth hostel nearby. A golf course for the less energetic!

St Justinian's (Porthstinian) - Castell Heinif - Penmaen Melyn - Porth Taflod - Porthlysgi - Porth Clais - Clegyr Boia - Rhosson - St Justinian's (Porthstinian)

OS Maps: 1:50 000 St David's and Haverfordwest 157; 1:25 000 Outdoor Leisure 35 North Pembrokeshire/St David's (Tyddewi) and Ramsey Island 1055 (SM 62/72).

Start: Coast Path at St Justinian's.

Access: St Justinian's — Porthstinian is the harbour for St Justinian's — is reached on the minor road from St David's. Follow the signposts! Nearest public transport access point at St David's.

Parking: St Justinian's.

Grade: Moderate — coastal path and some road walking.

Points of Interest:

1. St Justinian was the Breton friend and confessor of St David. During restoration work on the cathedral by Sir Gilbert Scott in the 1860's a number of bones were found embedded in mortar in a recess behind the High Altar. Transferred to an oak casket shortly after discovery it was believed until recently that they were the remains of St David, St Justinian, and the 12th century St Caradoc. However carbon dating by Oxford University in early 1997 has shown them to be all 11th or 12th century — a reprise at least for St Caradoc, to whom there is a shrine in the north transept of the cathedral. The ruins of St Justinian's chapel, now on private grounds, were rebuilt in the 16th century by Bishop Vaughan. St Justinian's Well is close by.

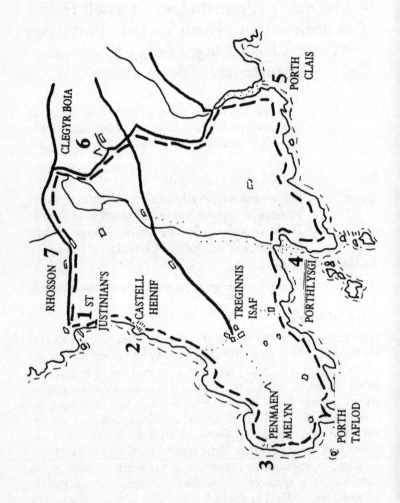

Porthstinian is home to the St David's lifeboat. The station, with it's distinctive red roof, was erected in 1911-12. The first vessel to grace the treacherous waters of Ramsey Sound was the *Augusta*, in 1869. Most treacherous are a series of rocks jutting into the Sound. Aptly named the Bitches, tides can rip through here at 7 knots, as many a ship has found to it's detriment. However it is this danger that is courted by the white water enthusiast in canoe or inflatable. A notice in the station, which can be visited, proudly states 300 lives saved. There is an older brick station dating from the 19th century at the base of the stone steps.

The harbour is well used. Ramsey Island is an RSPB (Royal Society for the Protection of Birds) nature reserve which can be visited by boat from Porthstinian from Easter to October 31. Alternative trips also leave from here for trips around the island. There is a breeding colony of seals. Cliffs colonisers include razorbills, guillemots, fulmars and kittiwakes. Gannets, shearwaters and puffins are regularly sighted. A popular embarkation point also for canoeists and divers, as well as the many pleasure and fishing craft moored here. Acting as the harbour for Ramsey Island, cattle and sheep were once landed to be driven to Haverfordwest fair, or on to Fishguard and Cardigan. There was a monastery on the island, reputedly founded by St Devynog in the 2nd century, as well as 2 cells, one of which belonged to St Justinian. St David and St Patrick are said to have met on the island.

2. There is a natural arch in the red sandstone peninsula here. The peninsula is backed by the impressive Iron Age fort of Castell Heinif. The 2 embankments, divided by a well excavated ditch, are skirted by the Coast Path. Good views of the twin hills and cliffs of Ramsey Island.

Saints and Sinners

A strong ascetic St Justinian retired to Ramsey Island to escape the lax mainland ways. However he soon became tired of the endless stream of visitors coming to pay him respects. Seeing solitude as the necessary requirement for direct access to God he accordingly took an axe and chopped away the rock causeway to the mainland, leaving instead a series of ferocious tidal rocks known as the Bitches.

This kind of saintly behaviour did nothing to endear him to his disciples, who replied in similar vein. They too took an axe, and, unkindly, chopped off his head. Quite unrepentant St Justinian picked up his head and walked across to the mainland. He put down his head and was buried on the site of his now ruined chapel.

* * *

3. The 19th century saw 2 attempts to mine copper here, at the westernmost tip of Wales. Both were as a result of agreements with the then owners of Treginnis Isaf Farm. The first occasion saw 2 Scottish brothers at the site in 1827. Mine buildings were erected, shafts sunk, and an adit driven across the peninsula. Their remains are clearly visible. A handful of local miners were employed, however lack of success led to closure in 1836. The second attempt dates from the 1870s when the shaft at Porth Taflod, seen as a more profitable site, came into use. Using a method common to many of Mid Wales' smaller mines men and materials were hoisted in a bucket connected by rope to a hand operated winch to the side of the shaft. The usual load of ore lifted was 1 cwt. There were no buildings erected on site. Following a fatal accident in 1883 the mine was closed, never to re-open. As a result of this accident 2 miners of the 5 on site were charged with manslaughter, but were later acquitted. The shaft is still visible, fenced off by the side of the Coast Path, with a soil heap close by. Treginnis Farm now operates as a farm for city children. The eagle-eyed may have noticed rusting winding gear and a small concrete quay in Carn y Wig bay, just before the Coast Path turns towards Penmaen Melyn. Nothing to do with the mine however, this was built in the 1920s for boats from the island farm.

4. Lysgi was a 6th century Irish chieftain who reputedly slew Boia, a fellow Irish chief who had his settlement nearby at Clegyr Boia. It was at Porth Lysgi that the *Augusta*, St David's first lifeboat, was housed until the slipway at Porthstinian was completed. The ruins

of the old station are still visible at the head of the beach. As at Porthstinian there was some ferrying of animals to and from Ramsey Island. There was trouble here in 1770 for the revenue cutter *Pelham*, at anchor. 3 Irish smuggling vessels were on their way in. With a combined crew of 80 men there was little chance for the *Pelham*. She was boarded, and found the next day wrecked on the fearsome rocks of Ramsey Island. *Pelham's* crew, however, had managed to save themselves.

5. Porth Clais has always been the harbour for St David's, and was at one time under the ownership of the church. Cathedral records show coal and limestone being landed here as early as 1384. Later imports included general merchandise and timber from Ireland, with exports of corn, malt and wool. Bristol became a much favoured port of call — with local corn going to help feed the city's growing population. Ships, most with purpose built flat bottoms, would have been beached here and their cargoes unloaded onto waiting carts. The breakwater, possibly Norman in origin, was extensively repaired in the 18th century. The limekilns on the old trading quays would have been in constant use. The limestone burnt in the kilns was taken by horse and cart for spreading on the fields, and for use as mortar. Lime as mortar was used in the construction of the cathedral, though the lime for this would probably have been burnt in kilns at the cathedral site. The restored kilns here are accompanied by a sign indicating their constant use from 1650 to 1900.

As well as providing a safe haven for trade and shelter Porth Clais' natural harbour was favoured by the occasional marauding Norseman, intent on sacking St David's semi-monastic settlement. The Mabinogion, that gem of medieval Welsh tales, notes Porth Clais as the landing place of the mythical boar, Twrch Trwyth, hotly pursued by Arthur. Later more materialistic ages would have seen the odd smuggler or two, often combining his activities with legitimate trade. The last imports to the harbour were of coal, required up to the 1950s to supply the city's gasworks, now demolished, and which stood on the site of the present car park. The inlet is still a busy place, popular now with the outdoor enthusiast, whether water borne or rock climber.

St David was born nearby, 1.25 miles/2 kilometres around the coast towards Solva, on the site now occupied by St Non's chapel. It is said that St Non's Well sprang forth at his birth. St Non, the saint's mother, went to Brittany shortly after the birth. Her tomb is in the chapel of Dirinon in Finistère. His father was reputed to be Sant, a Ceredigion chief. St David was baptized at a spring, now overgrown, to the north of the present car park, by Elvis — no, not the singer, but the then Bishop of Munster! David himself travelled widely before establishing his community. He helped to establish centres at Glastonbury, Bath and Gloucester, and, according to legend, travelled to Jerusalem in the company of other local saints where he was given an altar stone by the Patriarch.

6. Boia, he who was slain by Lysgi, was a contemporary of St David who built his fort on the rock outcrop overlooking the peninsula. Built in the early Iron Age tradition, stone faced ramparts would have enclosed the hill top. The gate, sited on the western slope, was found on excavation to have guard recesses on it's inner side. Legend has it that Boia's wife taunted St David and the local monks by having her maids disport themselves 'with bodies bare'. St David was not a saint without reason! The site of Clegyr Boia would have been in constant use over a period of thousands of years. Archaeologists have made a reconstruction of a Neolithic house built on the hill. Set between 2 rock walls, it's wooden roof was supported by 8 timber posts. Well worth taking the short track to the summit for the superb views of the landscape, with the cathedral tucked away safely in the valley of Merry Vale.

7. Rhosson Farm has a fine example of a medieval conical Flemish chimney. There is a disused well opposite. Rhosson was the birthplace of local historian Richard Fenton, friend of Dr Johnson, best known for his 1811 book, an 'Historical Tour through Pembrokeshire'.

Walk Directions: [-] denotes Point of Interest

1. Starting from St Justinian's [1] take the Coast Path leading off left at the top of the steps leading down to the lifeboat station.

2. Follow the Coast Path on to Castell Heinif [2] and continue straight ahead. Ignore the footpath leading inland — signposted just past the rock outcrops of Carn Goch — as this will take you inland to Treginnis Isaf.

3. Continue on to Penmaen Melyn [3] — there is another footpath just past the old mine workings leading inland, also to Treginnis Isaf.

4. Follow the Coast Path past Porth Taflod and Porth Henllys (another footpath inland to Treginnis Isaf), and on to Porth Lysgi [4]. Again another footpath leading inland. Continue on to Porth Clais [5].

5. At Porth Clais take the road leading directly ahead and uphill to meet a crossroads. Go straight ahead, passing Clegyr Boia [6] on your right, and continue to a T junction with the St David's to St Justinian's minor road.

6. Turn left onto the minor road and continue, passing Rhosson [7], to arrive back at St Justinian's and the starting point.

Facilities:

Parking also possible at Porth Clais car park.

Public toilets and emergency telephone at Porth Clais, camp site at Porth Clais Farm. Caravan park at St Justinian's. Boats for Ramsey Island leave from Porthstinian; there is a small booking office on site — no other facilities, unless you require the services of the lifeboat!

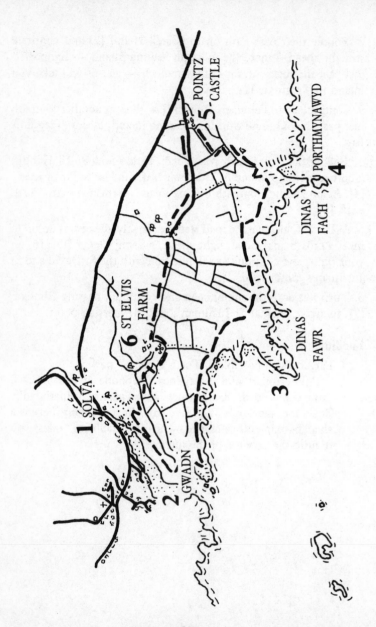

1 SOLVA
2 GWADN
3 DINAS FAWR
4 PORTHMYNAWYD
DINAS FACH
5 POINTZ CASTLE
6 ST ELVIS FARM

Solva - The Gribin - Gwadn - Dinas Fawr - Dinas Fach - Porthmynawyd - Pointz Castle - Lochvane - St Elvis Farm - Solva

OS Maps:	1:50 000 St David's and Haverfordwest 157; 1:25 000 Outdoor Leisure 35 North Pembrokeshire/St David's (Tyddewi) and Ramsey Island 1055 (SM 62/72), Newgale and Wolf's Castle 1056 (SM 82/92).
Start:	Car park in Lower Solva.
Access:	Solva is 2.5 miles/4 kilometres south-east of St David's on the A487 St David's to Newgale and Haverfordwest main road. Bus 411 stops at Solva.
Parking:	Free car park in Lower Solva.
Grade:	Moderate — mostly coastal path, field, farm track and minor road.

Points of Interest:

1. Solva's delightful setting makes it one of the most popular villages in the county. It's sheltered harbour, despite a dangerous entrance, has made it St Brides Bay's safest port of call. There has been much speculation over the origins of the name. Those who favour Norse origins point out that in Norse *sölv ö* can mean silver island, or *sol vo* a sunny harbour or fjord, as well as *sölva*, samphire. However the earliest references are to Salfach, closer to Solva's Welsh name of Solfach. Solva's recorded importance as a trading and commercial centre really begins in the 17th century with exports of wheat and malt, and imports of timber, cloth and oar blades. With the establishment of a shipping company in 1756 Solva entered it's period of prosperity. Unlike near neighbour Porth Clais, which could only handle vessels up to 100 tons, Solva could cater for ships of 500 tons, and by 1800 there were some 30

vessels of 20 to 250 tons here, as well as the beginnings of a shipbuilding industry. There were 9 warehouses built to house corn and butter for export to particularly Bristol, though also to Ireland, and coal and limestone were brought in to fertilize the corn basket of St David's peninsula.

The restored limekilns at the head of the beach (the rectangular section being the former lime burner's hut) contributed their share of lime for the fields. Richard Fenton, Pembrokeshire's historian, describes the effect of 2 of Solva's former 11 kilns 'whose hot vapour and dust and noise incident to them, make them very offensive, proving a great drawback on a residence on that part of the town where the chief shops and warehouses are . . . ' Trade had peaked by the mid 19th century, and with the coming of the railways quieter (until tourism!) and less polluted times were ahead for Solva. The last regular boat service to Bristol was finally discontinued in 1914.

Solva was host to the construction of 2 lighthouses for the Smalls, 2 notorious rocks projecting out into the Irish Sea to the west of Grassholm Island's gannet colony. The first, a curious shed like affair resting on iron and oak stanchions, was constructed in the 1770s to a design by a Liverpool violin maker, Henry Whitesides. He had been the winner of a competition launched by a group of Liverpool merchants who had become frustrated at the loss of Liverpool ships on the Smalls and the reefs of the nearby Hats and Barrels. A new lighthouse of Bodmin granite was chipped and dressed on the purpose built Trinity Quay, and taken out by tug for assembly on site in 1861. Trinity Quay was home to the Solva lifeboat, the *Charles and Mary Egerton*, from 1869 until 1887, when she was sold; the St David's lifeboat being preferred. The former lifeboat station, however, has found new uses.

2. Gwadn is Solva's beach. Despite the pebble ridge there is a fine expanse of golden sand at low tide. From here the nature of the difficulties facing anyone entering Solva's sheltered harbour become apparent, for guarding the entrance are St Elvis and Black Rocks. There was, until comparatively recently, a pilot to assist visiting vessels, and leading marks were painted on the 2 rocks, with 2

further marks inland. In 1882 Black Rock the major obstacle, was painted white with lime to assist returning mariners! Despite the dangers wrecks have been rare; perhaps the worst disaster concerned the *Phoebe and Mary*, en route from Philadelphia to Liverpool in 1773. Despite rescue by a Solva boat the returning vessel struck Black Rock with the loss of 60 lives, including 7 Solva men. One transatlantic vessel with a happier fate was the *Cradle*, which sailed from Solva in 1848 direct to New York for the princely sum of £3! The Gribin — possibly named from 'crib', the Welsh for ridge — divides the 2 valleys of Solva and the Gribin stream, that of Solva being the deeper, and, like the Milford Haven, a classic example of a drowned valley. There was an Iron Age fort on Gribin Point, with a settlement further inland, overlooking Lower Solva.

3. Rather difficult to believe now but the headland here at Dinas Fawr was mined for lead and silver for some 2 and a half centuries. No doubt there was some surface mining during the Bronze Age, but the first real attempt to mine below the surface dates from the 1620s. Operating as St Elvis Lead Mine there were further attempts until final failure in 1869. Ore extracted during the late 18th century was taken down to Gwadn where the then owner, Thomas Williams, had his storehouse. Most of the tunnels and adits are now sealed, but there are visible spoil heaps and levels adjacent to the Coast Path. There are sandy beaches close by, at Aber-west and Porth y Bwch, but access is problematic — though I have seen a fox ambling down the cliff without too much trouble!

4. Dinas Fach is an impressive narrow promontory jutting out into St Brides Bay. It is fronted by a turf covered island with the attractive sand beach of Porthmynawyd to one side. Rarely crowded in summer! The short springy turf of the headland is ideal feeding territory for those rarities of the crow family, the choughs, with their distinctive black coats and red beak and legs. The coastal section above Stacen y Brenin (the King's Stack), between Dinas Fawr and Dinas Fach, is ideal for the linnets, who congregate here in their red and chestnut finery during the summer months.

5. Pointz Castle, of which only the motte, or mound, survives, is

believed to take it's name from Poncius, a 12th century Norman knight and tenant of the then Bishop of St David's, Peter de Leia. Much of the land here would once have been the property of the bishop. Early Norman castles would have been simple affairs. The motte, a flattened mound of earth surrounded by a ditch, would have a wooden watchtower protected by a circular palisade of pointed stakes. Connected to it was the bailey, or court, similarly protected by ditch and fence, where the living quarters and stables would be housed. These wooden castles gradually gave way to the great stone castles which heralded Norman overlordship.

6. The 2 St Elvis cromlechau, or burial chambers, date back some 5,000 years. Used by Neolithic peoples for collective burials they would have originally been covered by earth or stones to form a barrow. Long after their purpose had been forgotten they became the subject of legend and prophecy. Graves of giants and heroes, it was said that if you were to walk around one on the night of the full moon you would see the face of your lover! To sleep in one meant madness, or the silver tongued gift of poetry. The word cromlech seems to have been first used by Pembrokeshire's Elizabethan historian, George Owen, 'crwm llech' meaning curved stone. Often the Breton term, dolmen (stone table), is used to describe them. There was at one time a chapel dedicated to St Teilo close by, though by the late 18th century it had fallen into disuse. However the font has been rescued, saved from it's new use as a pig trough!

Walk Directions: [-] denotes Point of Interest

1. Start from the car park in Lower Solva [1]. Cross the footbridge over the stream.

2. Join the Coast Path, either as it ascends the Gribin above the barred tunnel (constructed in the 1950s to carry materials for the construction of a treatment works in the neighbouring valley!), or above the limekilns at the head of the beach.

3. Continue along the Gribin to the beach at Gwadn [2]. Alternatively, if the tide is well out, it is possible to walk on the sand around to Gwadn from the starting point.

4. From Gwadn continue on the Coast Path across fields to Dinas Fawr [3].

5. Continue on to Dinas Fach and the sheltered sandy beach of Porthmynawyd [4].

6. From Porthmynawyd leave the coast and head inland on a clearly defined path.

7. Just past a ruined cottage on the right turn left and cross a stream by a footbridge and ascend to a field. This is a diversion to the route marked on the OS maps (other than Outdoor Leisure), but it is clearly waymarked.

8. Cross the stile into the field and keeping to the right field edge continue to reach a field gate and stile on the right. Cross the stile, and keeping to the left edge, continue ahead to a kissing gate.

9. Turn left and shortly cross a stile to reach the road at Pointz Castle [5]. Turn left and continue to Lochvane.

10. At Lochvane continue ahead to reach a green lane — the bridleway right leads to the main A487.

11. Continue on green and farm lanes to reach the farm lane to St Elvis Farm. Just before the farm buildings turn left, cross 2 stiles, and continue on the path fenced off from the farm track.

12. Just before a stile turn right through a wooden gate — the fenced-off area directly in front, right, protects St Elvis' cromlechau [6].

13. Continue ahead on a farm track. A short distance past a farm gate and stile there is another stile on the right. Choice here of continuing on the farm track to Gwadn, and back to Solva along the Gribin, or of bearing right and continuing across the field.

14. If turning right, cross the stile, and keeping to the right field edge, shortly cross another stile.

15. Turn immediately left and go through the wooden gate ahead, and continue along the wooded valley slope.

16. After a short distance the path emerges into more open scrubland. Bear right and continue downhill to reach the stream.

17. Cross the stream by a wooden footbridge and bear diagonally left. Continue uphill on a zig zag path to reach the Gribin at a wooden gate and stile.

18. Either continue across the stile onto the Gribin, to shortly bear right and downhill to Solva and the starting point, or bear right before the stile, keep to the left field edge and shortly bear left downhill, also to Lower Solva.

Facilities:

   Limited parking also possible at Pointz Castle.
   All facilities available in Solva. Middle Mill, just north of Solva, has both a woollen and a corn mill.